# I'm Just Sitting on a Fence

*The secrets of life.*

A Self-Help Memoir

by

Dax Flame

[Note: The story this memoir tells takes place over a period of about sixteen months.]

Lying in bed that morning and distracting his mind from the spider bite/poison ivy rash on his collarbone by trying to figure out an introduction for his book—which he'd been writing for sixteen months now and had seen evolve into many different shapes in that time—Timothy thought of this sentence and knew it'd be all right.

He lifted his right hand to his collarbone and prodded the bite/rash delicately. Very itchy, but he would not scratch it. Instead, Tim placed his hands on his face, took a deep breath in through the nose, decided to concentrate on his breathing, and exhaled warmly against his palms. After four more breaths, the irritation of the bite/rash had become less overwhelming. He removed his hands from his face, pulled the covers away from his body, and stepped out of bed. On his feet he wore grey ankle-socks, and around his waist he wore only green boxer-briefs, but he knew that no one was home, and so, scantily dressed as he was, he walked downstairs to the computer room, removed his notebook from his laptop case, and scribbled down the introductory sentence he'd just thought up.

He returned his notebook to the case and then pet his mom's German Sheppard, which was lying at his feet.

"Up girl. Up. Up. Outside. Outside."

He rubbed the black and blonde fur on her head and repeated the commands. She did not move, so he repeated them again, clapping his hands this time, and the dog rose to her feet and trotted through the house to the back door. Timothy followed, let her outside, closed the door behind her, and then turned and walked across the kitchen to the pantry. He removed a bag of rolled oats and another bag of dried figs. The oven-clock said it was ten o'clock. He boiled some water, chopped the figs, poured the water over the oats, and then began to eat his fig-oatmeal breakfast.

"Are you in line?" asked the fair-skinned little boy with the red hair and plaid Easter shirt.

Timothy was standing pretty far from the librarian's desk—four or five feet away—which was probably why the boy was unsure.

"Yeah, but you can go ahead."

"Oh, that's okay. I'll be quick."

As the boy moved to stand behind Timothy, Timothy turned to him, held up the books his mother had asked him to turn in, and said, "I just don't know what to do with these."

"Oh," said the boy, looking first at the books and then up at Timothy's face. Timothy noticed the boy glance sideways, towards the left side of the librarian's desk, and figured the boy probably knew where to turn them in.

He'd figured right. The boy looked back to Timothy and, pointing past the librarian's desk to where he'd just glanced, said, "You can turn books in right there."

Timothy turned, scanned the wall, and then saw the slot with the sign that read 'Books' above it.

"Oh, thank you."

The boy smiled at Timothy, and Timothy walked over and dropped the books in the slot.

When Timothy turned back around and started across the library towards the reading room, he noticed that the little boy was still smiling at him. And on the boy's smiling face Timothy observed a look of hesitant pride, probably caused by the fact that he'd just helped someone so much older than him.

"Thank you," Timothy said, giving a humble thumbs-up. "Thanks a lot."

"You're welcome."

"Yeah, I've never rented books from here before."

"Oh yeah... Um, I have."

"Cool. Well... Thank you. Thanks a lot."

As Timothy walked on, he glanced over his shoulder to observe the boy's face one more time. The smile—though somewhat faded—and the pride were still there, but the hesitance seemed to be gone.

Tim walked into the reading room and saw that all the chairs next to the outlets were occupied. One of these chairs was occupied by a well-dressed female with very pretty legs/hair. Timothy could not see her face from his angle, so he walked a few feet to the left, got a look at it, and confirmed that it was as pretty as he'd thought it might be. Her hair was some type of brown, though he did not know what type of brown to call it. "Auburn maybe..." he thought. "Oak... Or would you call it chestnut?" He looked at the girl another moment, and then he left the reading room to search for another chair where he could sit, plug in his laptop, and type.

He found a chair just like this in the Teen Zone. He sat, plugged in his laptop, opened the Word document he'd written his book's introduction in the day before, and began to re-read it.

It was a fourteen paragraph introduction that described that morning's routine, as well as the rest of his day—which he'd spent writing at the library—and after reading about half of it, he knew it was too dull to leave unaltered.

Timothy closed his eyes and thought about what could be done. At first he could think of nothing. He re-read the intro. He liked the first four paragraphs, but that was it. He dropped his face into his hands and thought harder.

He heard footsteps, and then, "That's not superman."

He raised his face from his hands and turned in his chair to see a little boy, probably about nine years old, with denim shorts, thick eyeglasses, and a bowl cut, looking at a magazine on the magazine rack with a cartoon of Dwight Howard dressed as Superman on the cover. Timothy stared at the boy, still thinking about what to do with his intro, and after about one minute, the boy walked away because he didn't know why Tim was staring at him. When he noticed that the boy was walking away, Timothy snapped out of it and realized that he'd been staring.

He laughed to himself, embarrassed, and turned to his laptop. As he stared into the screen his mind told him just what he had to do. He would delete all but the paragraphs that he liked—the first four—and he would have another go at the intro, writing this time about today's experiences at the library instead of yesterday's.

He did just this, and by the time he got to this sentence he felt pretty good.

"Does it need anything else," he wondered.

"Not really." The first sentence had pretty much said everything the intro really needed to say, so he decided he'd copy, paste, and italicize

4

it at the bottom of the Word document, and that'd be that.

*Lying in bed that morning and distracting his mind from the spider bite/poison ivy rash on his collarbone by trying to figure out an introduction for his book—which he'd been writing for sixteen months now and had seen evolve into many different shapes in that time—Timothy thought of this sentence and knew it'd be all right.*

How to read this book.

The aim of this book is to help the reader to improve his or her life.
Primarily through lesson-teaching essays about my own life, the reader will learn invaluable things (from the benefits of a positive out-look, to sticking up for oneself, to simply curing boredom the right way), and will gain a greater understanding of life.
The reader can use the lessons taught by my experiences like tools. When the reader finds his or herself in a similar situation or experienc-ing a similar experience to one of the ones I write about, he or she can recall how I handled the situation (the mistake or positive choice I made in my experience), and use this knowledge to help him or her navigate their situation to the best of their abilities.
This book can also guarantee to help educate the reader about the world, expand their mind, and deliver them a pleasurable reading ex-perience.
Hopefully you, the reader, will also come to know me, the author, a bit better during this process.
I recommend you to read this book when you are in a neutral mood (but you may do whatever you prefer). I believe that those who submit themselves fully to the book will yield the best results.

# Brushing Kevin's Hair

*A lesson on how not to do favors and the right way to cure boredom.*

One day, in my junior year of high school, our English teacher re-arranged the desks in the classroom and gave us new assigned seats. I was put behind the kid named Kevin.

Class started, and the teacher sat at the front of the class and read Shakespeare to us from the textbook. I wasn't in the mood, found it kind of boring, and could not keep my attention focused on the story. I began to look around, just daydreaming and such. Then I looked at the back of Kevin's head in front of me. I saw that his black hair was quite a mess, and I had nothing else to do, so I got my comb from my pocket and decided to run it through his hair. He was jumpy and turned around the second it touched his head. He just looked at me. I looked at him. He seemed like he wanted to say something, but turned back around. As I looked at his hair, I decided to see if I could pluck a single strand of it out of his head without him noticing. I spotted a hair sticking out nicely, brought my hand to it, slowly squeezed my fingers around it, and then yanked it out.

He didn't notice. I put the hair on my textbook and played with it for a minute, then decided to try to neaten his hair again. I lifted my comb, brought it to the back of his head, and once again, he jumped at the touch and spun around. This time he looked at me and whispered, so the teacher wouldn't hear him, "Why are you touching my head?"

"I was just trying to comb your hair. It's pretty messy," I told him.

"Well, it's fine, don't touch it," he whispered and turned back around.

He seemed like he didn't want me to comb the hair for him, but I also thought he might be playing coy, so I told myself I'd give it one more go, and if he objected again I'd find something else to do. So I lifted the comb back to his head and brought it down through the hair as I had before. Once again he whipped around at the touch, and this time he looked unmistakably angry when he whispered, *"Seriously.* Quit. Touching. My. Hair." He stared at me waiting for me to say 'okay'.

"No," I said, I don't know why, probably out of boredom.

"Stop touching my freaking hair or I'll break your d*mn comb," he whispered more loudly, looking at me another moment, and then turning back around.

I felt sorry for him, and also bored. I could tell he was tense, so I decided I'd give him a massage. I put my comb in my pocket, reached out, placed my hands on his shoulders, and barely got one squeeze in before I heard him say, not whisper, "My god!" as he twisted around, slapped my hand (he was trying to get my comb to destroy it), and then ferociously looked up at my face when he saw the comb wasn't there. His face was red, and I couldn't tell what he was going to do. He looked like he wanted to hit me, but instead he grabbed my textbook and slammed it shut.

"You just squished your hair," I told him as I remembered the hair I'd placed on the page. Before he could respond, the teacher said, "What is going on?" as she and most of the class looked at us.

"He won't keep his hands off me. He keeps touching my head," Kevin immediately told her in a convincing, frustrated voice. She looked at me.

"No... I was trying to comb his hair, and then I was just trying to relax him because he seemed tense," I said. I didn't mention that his hair was a mess, because the whole class was listening.

"Really? You were trying to comb his hair while you're supposed to be reading along in your textbook...? You need to keep your hands to yourself, or I'm going to move you if you're not mature enough to handle a new seating arrangement," the teacher said, and let her gaze linger on me another moment before turning back to the textbook.

She'd embarrassed me in front of the class, made me feel small, and I didn't feel like reading, so as she looked for her place in the textbook, I said, "You won't be doing me any favors by keeping me in *this* desk." I was attempting to make a good comeback. It wasn't that great.

"Excuse me?" she asked, turning her attention back to me.

"Nothing, sorry," I said.

"No, you said something. Do you have something important you'd like to share with the class?" she said in an intimidating, 'I can send you to detention' tone.

"I didn't say *something*. I didn't say the *word* <u>something</u>," I said, just asking for it.

She stood up from her chair and said, "Come here," as she walked towards her desk. I already knew she was going to get a counseler's office slip, which of course meant detention and a phone call home.

I looked at Kevin, who was smiling, and mouthed the words '*thanks a lot*' as I walked by him on my way to the teacher's desk. But deep down I probably really knew it was my fault.

The teacher wrote out the slip. I got my backpack, loaded my textbook into it, and while I walked towards the door, I felt embarrassed as I saw the class's smirking faces. I opened the door and paused there in the doorway, looking at the class. The teacher asked, "Is there a problem?"

I glanced at her, and then looked at Kevin. "Kevin's a snitch!" I screamed and slammed the door. I ran to the counselor's office and received my punishment. I immediately regretted my actions.

So, did I learn from this punishment? I did. The next day when I returned to class, we were reading Shakespeare again, and again I found it unable to hold my attention. Instead of using Kevin to occupy my mind, I decided to entertain myself without causing any disturbances or bothering anyone else. I'd packed a deck of cards in my backpack that morning, and so as the teacher read to the class, I played solitaire on my desk. After class I apologized to the teacher for the way I'd acted, and she appreciated me doing so.

# Room in the Hot Tub

*A lesson on persistence.*

Eventually music loses its flare when you're driving solo across the country. By the time I reached Miami I was dead tired of the car and ready to stretch my legs. I parked in a garage about a block from my hostel, walked the block, checked-in, put away my bags, and went back downstairs to see if there was anyone around to listen to my day's story. There were plenty of people around. I approached a Latin man that appeared to be about forty and said, "Hi. Where are you from?" He was from Miami, and was the owner of this hostel. He seemed friendly, so I told him, "I actually just got my first speeding ticket when I was driving here."

He nodded, and in his eye I detected something like reproof, but I continued.

"I was just going five over. And I wasn't even meaning to. Actually, I was crying when the police officer came to my window, but he still gave me the ticket."

"You shouldn't have been speeding," the man said.

I didn't know how to reply to that. He clearly wasn't on my side. Instead of writing him off as unfriendly though, I assumed he must've had some bad history with a speeding driver, and I just nodded my head and left.

I walked from the lobby out to the courtyard, where there were twenty or so people hanging out, talking. The hot tub caught my eye. After the long day driving, that's where I'd rest my bones. And in the tub was a young man and a young woman—two youths that'd certainly listen to my story, and possibly share a few of their own (maybe we'd even play some cards after talking—if we bonded enough).

I went upstairs and changed into my bathing suit. I fixed my hair in the mirror, brushed my teeth so clean that they almost bled, grabbed my towel, and returned to the courtyard, where there were three additional people now in the tub.

It was a small tub, and six people would be a tight squeeze. I wandered over towards it, and lingered around the outside, a few feet away, listening to their conversation. All three of the guys in the tub had British or Australian accents. One had blonde surfer hair and whiskers, one was African-American (but with an accent), and the other had a thin, pale body and short, brown hair. There was a girl with blonde hair and a green bathing suit next to that one, and the other girl was a brunette with a charming face and a white bathing suit, and she was sitting beside the guy with blonde surfer hair. The content of their conversation made them seem like young, hip partiers, and that was all right with me.

"I'm just gonna rest my towel right here if that's all right..." I said as I laid my towel on the outer ledge of the tub. They looked up at me, two of those guys nodded that it was all right, and they continued their conversation. I sat on the ledge next to my towel, and turned my body towards them a little so that I could eventually work my way into the conversation. But I could find no openings, and so I just singled out the brown-haired guy and asked him where he was from. Australia. I told him I was from the U.S. I asked about his trip, then I asked the African-American guy where he was from. The U.K. indeed. I repeated that I was from the U.S., and then I turned all the way towards the group so that I could put my legs in the water. When I did this, all of them were looking at me, so I asked, "Do you want to hear about a speeding ticket I got today?"

They said sure, with a good amount of enthusiasm.

"Well, this morning, when I was driving here, I got pulled over for going seventy-five, and I was in a seventy. But I wasn't even trying to; like, I always just hit cruise control at the speed limit, so it was just an accident. And, um, when the cop pulled me over, I was actually crying—because it was my first ticket—and he just asked for my license and registration, and then went back to his car. So, when he was at his car, I drove away, because I didn't realize I was supposed to get them back—I was just thinking, 'Well, I guess I just got my first ticket.'"

They seemed to be interested in what I was saying, but at the same time I couldn't tell for sure if they really were.

I continued. "Well, then I see that he's driving in my rearview mirror again—I see the lights—and I thought, 'Wow, that was fast. He's already got another call.' Because I thought he was going after someone else. But he continues to drive behind me, and he won't pass me, even

11

though everyone else is driving the same speed as me, so I just rolled down my window and started waving for him to go around, but um, he wouldn't go around me..."

Although they tried to hide it, I could now see that they were definitely losing interest a little, even though I was getting to the best part. Still, I continued.

"So then I pulled back over, and he told me that in all his years he'd never had someone drive off without their license. So he gave me the ticket, and now I've just gotta pay like, a hundred dollars I think."

"Aw, that sucks," said the blonde guy.

"Yeah..." I agreed.

And then they were talking about something else. But at least I was still there with them, with my legs in the tub. As they talked I was able to add an occasional comment, and my calves felt pretty nice soaking in the water. Slowly throughout the conversation, gradually, I slid my legs more and more into the water, until they were in to about the knees. Then I asked the girl in the green suit if she'd mind scooting over a little. She just said, "Um..." and when I asked if she'd mind me sitting between her and the guy beside her—the one with the brown hair—the guy replied, "I don't think there's enough room, mate."

"Okay..."

The conversation continued. I was no longer listening. I was getting a little bored of not being fully in the water.

"Do you mind just scooting over a little bit?"

He looked back up. "There's really not enough room."

And the girl agreed, "Yeah... Sorry. We might be out soon though."

But the main idea was that I wanted to be in the tub at the same time as them.

"Can I go right there in the middle?" I asked a bit timidly.

"What do you mean?"

"Maybe I'll just kneel in the middle," I said, and pointed towards the middle part of the tub where their legs were resting but where there'd also be just enough space for me to kneel. They still didn't know what I meant, so I demonstrated. I stepped over the girl and guy into the middle of the tub, yelling a little as my body dropped into the water since it nearly burned my waist and stomach off.

And a second later the brown-haired guy and the green-bathing suit girl got up and left, and I was able to sit in their spot. The other three only stayed in about ten more minutes, but it was a good ten minutes in which I'd been able to participate a little more actively in the conversation, and my body became very relaxed from the water during that time. I stayed in for a little bit longer after they'd left, and then went to my room and watched 'Black Swan'.

This story provides me with a chance to speak on a quality that I'm a big supporter of—persistence.

Because I did not give up on sharing the story of my ticket after the hostel owner rebuked me, I came across the people in the hot tub, whom I was able to successfully share the story with. And then, when the people in the tub rejected my plea to join them, I did not turn away and leave, I waited patiently and then asked again. And upon being rejected the second time, I tried searching for a creative solution to the problem. That solution was to go into the middle of the tub, and even though it was imperfect, it ultimately worked out, because then the other two left and there was room for me to sit for ten nice minutes with the remaining three. Persistence means to not give up.

Other scenarios in which persistence is beneficial:

- When dealing with bumps in relationships.
- When trying to convince people of something.
- When chasing a goal.
- When in a sticky situation.
- When pursuing something.

It is important to sometimes take a break from the seriousness of life, and for this reason I have included three short works of fiction in this book, written solely to be enjoyed. (Each of these works does have some lesson within, but the lesson is just bonus.)

On the next page—page 15—you will find *Billy's Big Birthday*. (Written July 29, 2011.)

On page 64 is *Love and Death in the Cinque Terre*. (Idea conceived October 20, 2011. Written April 21, 2012.)

And on page 106 is *Lupis and the Erector*. (Written March 7, 2013.)

(You may also feel free to skip the fictions if you prefer.)

Thursday

Billy sat on the worn couch. He spent almost every waking minute of his life this way on that couch, save for those he spent eating in the kitchen on the floor, or relieving himself in the always finely trimmed grass of the back yard. Today was Thursday and Billy's 56th birthday was on Saturday. He looked forward to it, and although his parents and his brother never acknowledged it, he always treated himself in his own special way, such as eating some of his brother's breakfast from the table or chewing on one of the legs of a wooden dining chair, even if it did get him shoved and whacked or kicked. But today was Thursday, Saturday was two days away, and until then, Billy planned to sit on the worn couch.

So he sat as planned for a good half hour or so until his brother woke up and decided that he wanted to smash his book sack into Billy's back. So his brother did this and then Billy, in pain, returned to sitting, not complaining, as this had become part of their morning routine.

Billy's brother, Jacob, was seven years old. Their parents treated him like a prince, bathing him with the most extravagant bathing salts once a day, feeding him more goose, caviar, and quail at each meal than two full grown men could eat, and dressing him in outfits that would have made the Queen of England shed a jealous tear. Billy cried every night, just before bed, thinking of the outfits. Jacob was a thin boy of average seven-year-old height, a bit taller than Billy, and although he was skinny, he had sausage shaped fingers. If one were to look Jacob in the eye, they would see the devil dancing and laughing in his pupil. He was also allergic to mirrors, so the Robins family never kept one in the house. Jacob and Billy were both born on August 14th 1938. They joined Mr. and Mrs. Robins' life on the same day. Jacob joined by exiting Mrs. Robins' womb, and Billy through adoption. Now you may notice that this math does not add up, Billy being fifty-five years old and Jacob seven, but Billy was a dog, you see, he just did not know it yet.

So, Billy sat and watched from the couch, like he did every morning, as his parents and Jacob ate their breakfast at the dining table, Mrs. Robins occasionally wiping a crumb from the corner of Jacob's mouth and Mr. Robins alternating between combing his own thick head of hair and his darling son's. Billy often wondered why he wasn't ever allowed a breakfast, his parents thought he should only be fed once every night, but deep down he couldn't understand why. The Robins' finished their breakfast, and on their way out the door to drop Jacob off at school before heading to work, Billy overheard a conversation between Mr. and Mrs. Robins that he noticed was about him. He listened closely and heard his name mentioned a few times, in addition to something about Jacob being dissatisfied, someone named Ashleigh arriving Friday night, and them putting something to sleep before this Ashleigh person arrived. They made their way out of the house, shutting and locking the door behind them.

Billy sat alone in the quiet living room. He thought about what the meaning of the conversation could have been. Friday was tomorrow. His and Jacob's birthday was Saturday. The only other time he'd heard Mr. and Mrs. Robins talk about putting something to sleep before was when they were referring to his birth mother being euthanized the day she gave birth to him. "Could they be planning to euthanize me?" He asked himself out loud. "No, I'm a good son, I've never done anything that would lead my parents to do such a horrible thing." Billy tried not to panic, he tried to believe what he'd told himself, but his parents had been extra cold to him lately, and Jacob did seem to be growing bored with hitting him. Soon speculation got the best of him and he began to have a full on panic attack. He hopped off the couch and paced the living room as he tried to think of what could be done. His mind raced and soon the anxiety was too much to bear, he began to black out and had to take a seat. There was nothing he could do, he decided. His parents never left a door unlocked when they weren't at the house, and anytime they let him outside, they tied a rope to his necklace so he couldn't run away. Plus, even if he did manage to escape, Billy had never been beyond the backyard before, how could he know if he'd be able to make it more than even a day out in the real world. "I am going to die tomorrow, Friday, August 13th, and there's nothing I can do about it." He returned to the couch where he sat and wept until the early evening, when his parents and Jacob returned home.

Mrs. Robins prepared supper and Mr. Robins gave Jacob his daily back rub as they discussed his upcoming birthday. "I think you'll be very pleased with your present on Saturday Jacob." Billy heard Mr. Robins whisper into his son's ear. "Well Christ Almighty, I should hope so father, have you forgotten that Saturday is my Birthday after all?" Jacob snapped back. "Of course not Jacob—and that is why I think you'll be very delighted come Saturday..." Mr. Robins said, smiling, as he turned to wink at his wife, Mrs. Robins, in the kitchen, "Now take a deep breath, lay back down, and relax. I've still got about four more minutes to go on your lower back."

Watching this exchange only furthered Billy's belief that his suspicions were true. He was positively sure of it now. But he felt nothing. He was numb. He felt nothing because he knew he could do nothing.

Mr. and Mrs. Robins ate their dinner, unusually giddy with excitement, before giving Jacob a glass of warm milk and laying him down for bed. Billy lay on the couch as his parents arrived from Jacob's room discussing Jacob's request, or demand rather, to be homeschooled, and which one of them would be quitting their job to so that they could honor the request. Mr. Robins, who had taken a seat on one end of the couch, began to remove his shoes and decided he'd like to lie down, but just as he was about to, he spotted Billy sitting on the other end. Without a second's hesitation, he put his right shoe back on and kicked Billy for all he was worth, sending him three feet into the air, and then falling back down, colliding violently against the coffee table before landing with a thud on the cold tile floor. He gasped for air, trying to catch his breath as he crawled desperately to the corner of the living room, where he sat down with a deep, stabbing pain in his side, and buried his head in his arms. Mr. and Mrs. Robins carried on their conversation, while Billy lay there whimpering, before his stomach growled and he realized that Mrs. Robins had forgotten to feed him. "I won't even be getting a last meal." He thought to himself.

It was decided that Mrs. Robins would quit her job to begin homeschooling Jacob. "Oh Jacob will be *so* delighted. This news will make a lovely addition to his present on Saturday!" Mr. Robins nearly shouted, running his hands through his marvelous jet-black hair, looking as if he could burst from excitement at any moment. "Oh Walter, I agree!" Mrs. Robins said before continuing, "So let me tell you what I was thinking the plan should be for tomorrow. We put Jacob to sleep at eight, the trainer will leave Ashleigh on the front porch at a quarter to nine…"

Mrs. Robins continued to talk, but Billy lost track of what she was saying. We put Jacob to sleep at eight? We put Jacob to sleep at eight. Of course! Jacob always went to bed at eight! In his paranoia Billy had forgotten that his parents always said they were going to 'lay Jacob down' or 'put him to sleep' or 'bring him to bed'. He wasn't going to be euthanized. He didn't know why they had mentioned his name earlier or who Ashleigh was, but he didn't care, he was going to live! He forgot about his hunger and the pain in his side, and as his parents talked, he drifted into a nice deep sleep, thoughts floating through his mind about what he'd do tomorrow, the first day of the rest of his life.

Friday

Billy woke up the next morning feeling like a new person. He woke up feeling that today was going to be a special day. Today he was going to kiss the sky. Instead of wobbling over and plopping down on the worn couch like he did every other day, he decided he wanted to jog around the living room, so he did. Then he decided he wanted to jog around the kitchen, and he did. He stopped for a moment when he noticed a great hunger in his stomach. He hadn't eaten in over twenty-four hours. But this didn't stop him. He felt a glorious new strength unlike any he'd ever felt before. He continued to jog around the rooms, happy as could be just to be alive.

Mr. Robins made his way into the kitchen where he sat and began to read the day's newspaper. Mrs. Robins followed closely behind, putting on her apron before starting to prepare breakfast. Jacob came not long after and sat at the table, ready to be served. Billy continued to jog unacknowledged. He didn't show any signs of fatigue. He was loving it. Jacob was first to notice the jogging. He was confused by the behavior. He stood up from his chair and watched. Not only was he confused by the behavior, but, he decided, he was also bothered by it. Jacob grabbed the newspaper from his dad's hands as he walked towards Billy, rolled it up tightly in his right hand and raised it high above his head. Billy stopped jogging and looked up at Jacob standing before him. He knew what was about to happen, for it'd happened so many times before, but, Billy felt that maybe today he didn't deserve to have the newspaper brought down upon his head. Maybe he should do something, he thought. Maybe he should stick up for himself. Billy saw Jacob's dangling left hand, and right as his brother began to swing the newspaper downward, Billy leapt at him, sinking his teeth deep into the dangling wrist. Jacob shrieked. Mr. and Mrs. Robins turned and came running. Billy ripped and chewed at the flesh and the left hand was quickly severed from Jacob's arm. Jacob passed out, falling backwards into his mother's arms as Mr. Robins yanked Billy up by the necklace and held him high in the air above his head. As Billy sat there suspended in the air, he felt as if he were floating, time seemed to stand still, and he couldn't help but feel proud of the fact that he'd just stood up for himself. He quickly realized that Mr. Robins was probably about to throw him to the ground or at a wall, and even though the hand had satisfied his appetite, he reached his face down and bit into Mr. Robins' head. Mr. Robins let go of Billy, yelling in pain, and Billy, teeth still deep in Mr. Robins' skin, fell quite hard to the ground, ripping Mr. Robins' scalp off in the process. Mr. Robins fell face first into the living room floor, fainting on the way down. Mrs. Robins, screaming, looked at Billy, and before she smacked him across the face, she stopped herself to study what she saw before her. For the first time since the day they adopted him, she really looked at Billy. She understood. She got down on her left knee and bowed to Billy. Her son. Billy approached her and gently kissed her hand, sending the glorious shiver of forgiveness up her spine.

Billy surveyed the room, his father, Walter Robins, and his brother, Jacob Robins, both laying on the ground unconscious, and his mother, Bef Robins, bowing gracefully, and soon an uncontrollable sense of great pride washed over him. He had done it, he'd stuck up for himself, and it was beautiful. Things would be different from now on; everyone in the house would treat each other both equally and respectfully. And when Mr. Robins and Jacob arose from their unconscious states, Billy knew that they would understand just as Mrs. Robins had.

Doctor West came to the house around a quarter past noon to stitch up Mr. Robins' head and fix Jacob's arm. Mr. Robins said he felt fine, but the doctor told him he would have to be bald for the rest of his life, and Jacob, who felt fine as well, had to have his right hand removed from his arm and replaced with a claw so it would match the new claw on the end of his left arm. Mrs. Robins sat nuzzled up to her husband on the couch, petting his hairless head to show him that she accepted him. Billy, on the other side of the room, watched and smiled a serene smile as he sat in Mr. Robins' one hundred percent rawhide recliner. Jacob, who had been unusually quiet, approached Billy. He stood in front of Billy, silent, before saying, "Thank you." Billy looked into Jacob's eyes, and in his pupil he could see a shooting star. Billy smiled and Jacob knew that even though he wasn't worthy, Billy forgave him. The moment was beautiful. Jacob was first to break the ice, saying "I would hug you but I don't want to stab you with my claws!" Billy and Jacob shared a great, uproarious laugh. Brothers. Things settled down, and then Jacob took off his beautiful multicolored coat, the best one he had, and placed it on Billy, "It's yours now." He told his brother. "I... I don't know what to say." Billy said as a tear of joy formed in his eye. Jacob stopped him, "I guess you can have these too. I don't think I'll be needing them anymore!" He said as he handed over a pair of gorgeous silk gloves. Everyone laughed as Jacob waved his claws in the air. "Oh boy, Jacob! Why can't you give me a hug? What am I an animal?" Billy yelled through his laughter. Everyone's hysterics quickly turned to silence. Billy looked around confused. "There's something we need to tell you." Mr. and Mrs. Robins said. "You are a dog." Billy stared at them blankly, not able to comprehend the meaning of the words that had just been spoken to him. "I'm a what? A dog...? What's that?" He asked. "An animal. It's an animal. You're an animal." The Robins' responded, "We're sorry, but we realized today you deserve to hear the truth. You're not a human. You're a dog. We're sorry. Also, we didn't know you could talk before today, and we think that's cool if it makes you feel any better." Billy looked around, studying their faces. An anger began to boil in the pit of his stomach. His heart pounded muscularly, and he felt as though he was going to vomit. But as he continued to gaze into their faces, he could tell that they weren't lying to him. They had too much of a newfound respect for him to pull something silly like that. "Okay, well thanks for telling me." He finally said as tears filled his eyes. Mr. Robins, Mrs. Robins, and Jacob looked at one another, nodded a knowing nod, and went to their rooms to let Billy have some time alone to digest the information.

Billy felt the same pride for sticking up for himself as he had before, but he was confused now. The joy that once pulsed through his veins had been drained, depleted, stolen, and now he was left wondering who, or what, he was. He walked over to the couch, head hanging low, and returned to the worn spot that he knew so well.

Mrs. Robins cooked a lovely feast for dinner, and she and Mr. Robins invited Billy to join them, but Billy just didn't have an appetite. They enjoyed their meal, washed up, and then laid Jacob down for bed. They came out of Jacob's room to tell Billy goodnight, something they had never done before today, and then went off to their room to retire for the night.

Billy sat in his spot, still trying to process the information he'd been told, for about a half hour or so before the doorbell rang. Everyone that usually answered the door was asleep, so it went unanswered. The doorbell rang again, and then one more time, and eventually the man outside decided he couldn't wait any longer, so he opened the door, placed a large box on the floor, closed the door and left. Billy eyed the box from the couch. It seemed usual enough, and since he didn't have the energy to investigate, he put his head back down. He began to doze off when he heard a sound come from the box's general direction. He glanced over at it and before long he heard the sound again. He was very curious now. Even a little worried, maybe. He hopped off the couch and approached the box. It smelled like nothing he'd ever smelt before, but in an unexplainable way that he actually seemed to enjoy. He slowly began to unwrap and open the box with his hands and teeth. It was rather difficult to rip the box, but when the job was complete, he saw before him the most beautiful creature he'd ever seen. "What are you?" Billy asked the creature. "I'm a dog." It said as it stared into his eyes. He looked at its necklace and saw a little golden circle with the word *Ashleigh* written across it. He also saw in the little golden circle something he'd never seen before. His reflection. He realized. He looked into her eyes, and she into his. They kissed each other with more passion than any human can ever even begin to imagine. They looked out the window right in time to see a magnificent display of fireworks, since there was a celebration being held in town that night. They returned to kissing each other as the crowd screamed and cheered, and I know, that if they had died that night, they would have died the two happiest dogs the world had ever known. "Don't you know, Billy, that you, are a shooting star?"

Saturday and Beyond

The next day Billy and Jacob shared the best Birthday either had ever had. Jacob loved getting Ashleigh, and Billy ate more cake than ever before. Billy and Ashleigh had puppies, and Mr. and Mrs. Robins had a set of triplets. The Robins family was happy, and better yet, no one ever hit Billy anymore. Of course, on occasion he might have had to bare his teeth for Mr. and Mrs. Robins to remind them of what he was capable of, but besides that it was smooth sailing. When you really get down to it, Billy was just a good-hearted dog with a beautiful soul who learned to stick up for himself, finding love along the way. And the Robins weren't so bad either. ; )

# The Hide and The Seek

*A lesson on having hope in frightful situations and the importance of informing people of your whereabouts.*

A plane was soaring through the blue sky. I watched it go, and go, and go, because I didn't want to do my homework. My mom was reading on the blanket she'd brought for the two of us, and I was lying in the grass beside it. It was a spring day in the seventh grade, and she had taken me to the park after picking me up from school just to get outside into the beautiful weather for a little bit.

About fifteen minutes after we'd arrived, a group of seven of my peers showed up. These peers were on the somewhat popular side. They were kids that I considered to be cool, and funny. There were five boys, and two very pretty girls.

The boys had some spirit in them. That's what I remember. They were rambunctious and I loved it. I watched as they horsed around for a bit, and then one of the boys broke away from the others to go sit on the ground and talk with one of the girls. The other four boys followed his lead shortly after, and went and laid on their stomachs in a circle with the other girl. I was thinking maybe I could go join them, maybe I'd go lay casually in the circle, but when I went to put my homework away I saw that five more kids, also from my grade level, were walking across the park towards the original seven. It was almost like a party. They all slapped high fives and greeted each other and laughed and seemed so happy to me. Amongst the new five was a crush of mine named Angela—very pretty. I remember them singing, "I get knocked down!—But I get up again!—Ain't never gonna keep me down!—I get knocked down! ..." and as they were singing it I put my homework and pencil away in my backpack, because the next time they sang, "I get knocked down!" I was planning to maybe go over and play-tackle or push one of them, jokingly, to break the ice and start a conversation and see if they wanted me to hang out.

So as I was telling my mom that I was gonna go say hi to some friends (and she said that that was all right, just so long as I promised to do my homework first thing when we got home) five or so of the peers got up and started doing something else. Angela was with them. One of the guys was up against the park fence, with his hands over his eyes, and the other four or so were running off, laughing. They were playing hide and seek. I wanted to swap lives with that boy counting against the fence. I watched that boy as he counted to whatever and then searched for the hiders. He found Garrett within seconds, and the others came out of their spots, laughing and stuff. And as Garrett went against the fence to count, I began across the park in his direction, making sure to watch exactly where everyone hid.

"I know where everyone hid. Follow me," I whispered into Garrett's ear, at the fence.

He looked at me, and he was confused, since he didn't know I was playing too.

"I know exactly where everyone hid. Follow me. Come on," I repeated, and lifted my pointer finger to my lips (the '*shh*' sign) to signal that it was a gift of sorts, a secret.

"Where's Angela?" were the very first words he asked.

I pointed down the fence where I'd seen her go, and told him, "In that bush. Come on," and we went running down to that bush to find her. Garrett tagged her and she came up laughing and I said, "Good job," to Garrett and then the others came out of their spots, and they were all talking, and that's when I asked if I could play. At first they didn't hear me, but when I asked a second time, a solid kid named John said yeah, sure, I could play, and he told the others I was gonna play.

Nothing could have made me happier.

I knew exactly where I'd hide.

And when Angela went down the fence to start her counting, I took off, laughing like the others, and sprinted farther than any of them—across the park, past the other fence, and behind the music building to where the AC units were. Then I got on my hands and knees and crawled in between the units and the wall—wedged myself in so that I'd be hardly visible. *They'll never find me here*, I thought to myself... And they never did.

I sat in that spot, absolutely giddy with excitement, for somewhere around a half hour. Thoughts of Angela's face and of how impressed everyone would be when they finally did find me sustained me as I sat squeezed up in that tight little spot. Maybe Angela would find me and

I'd go running and she'd have to tag me. And when she did, I imagined she would say, out of breath, "*Finally*. How did you even find that spot?" "Oh I just knew about it because we came here already a couple weeks ago. Don't worry about it," I'd reply. And she'd laugh and maybe say, "Well that was a really good spot, and it was so fun chasing you too. You're a good runner." And the other guys might say, "Yeah, that was really probably the best hiding spot anyone's ever found." And then, after imagining this, I'd giggle to myself, and then I'd wonder where in the park the group was right now—where they were searching for me—and I'd giggle again, and I'd wonder if I would be a part of the group after this, and then I'd imagine future activities I would enjoy with the group (soap box derbies, smores, romance galore, gossip, etc.).

It was probably a little after twenty or so minutes when I first began to notice the uncomfortableness of my spot. I suppose the initial rush of ecstasy I'd experienced was beginning to wear off, and as time ticked on I was becoming more ready to get active again. But I decided to stick with it, to wait for them, and stayed there for maybe five or ten more minutes, shifting positions constantly and hoping pretty badly that they'd soon find me. And then I decided I'd take a permanent break from the hiding and reveal myself to the seekers.

I crawled out from behind the AC unit, rose to my feet, and started towards the fence, walking proudly but cautiously. Before I actually revealed myself to them, I wanted to scope things out and see where the game was at to be sure that I was truly the last one hiding, since I supposed that it was possible that maybe Angela still hadn't found one or two of the other guys and was maybe still looking for me *and* them. So when I reached the fence, I peeked my head around it *slowly*. I glanced about quickly and withdrew my head before anyone could spot me. But I also wasn't sure if I'd spotted them. So I stuck my head back around, didn't see Angela upon quick inspection, and re-withdrew my head. I closed my eyes and analyzed the visuals from the two glances. Had I seen them? It'd been too quick to tell. I decided to risk taking another, longer look, poked my head around one more time, and kept it there as I looked out across the grass. I saw a few adults and such, but I saw none of my peers. I wondered, *Have they started a new game?*

*Are they all up and hiding?* But then I remembered that not all of my peers had been playing, so it wouldn't make sense for them all to be hiding. I was trying to make sense of this when something else struck me.

My mom... Where was she?

She was not sitting where I'd last seen her.

She was not anywhere in my sight.

She was not, apparently, at the park.

"What the heck is going on?"

And suddenly I felt panic looming on the wings of my brain, threatening to cripple and overtake me.

Because I did not know the way back home. And my mom had never left me anywhere before. And I didn't have a cell phone. And even if I did know the way home, I could not walk that far...

Death was the word that was in my mind.

The tears were imminent. My knees gave out beneath me.

Death.

And then something happened. Somewhere in the depths of my chest, an instinct told me that I had to rise. It told me to stand back up, to not wither away, to shout out. And I did. I screamed, "Mom!"

And then I screamed it again, louder, "*Mom!*"

The tears began to flow, and I screamed it a third and fourth time, "*MOM! ... MOM!*"

Then I heard a woman's voice coming my way, and I turned to see some female stranger looking at me, saying stuff. She was with a man. They were rising from their blanket, and had probably come to the park for a picnic.

They told me they'd seen my mom looking for me. They were acting like they wanted to help. But I knew about strangers, and I was in the most vulnerable position of my life. So I kept my distance from them. But then, I spilled my guts, because I felt I had no other choice but to trust them. I told them, sobbing, how me and my mom had been sitting on a blanket, then I went to see friends, then I'd hidden at the building forever, and when I'd come back she was gone... They said don't worry, don't worry, we'd find her. And suddenly, for some reason, I knew I could trust them, and panic relinquished its stranglehold on my

27

mind's throat, and while I did not exactly feel like I'd been completely rescued, and fear definitely still bubbled within, death no longer seemed like the unavoidable conclusion to this day.

I sat on the blanket with the woman, and the man was gonna go searching for my mom. They were both probably about thirty years old. The man was tall, and had a brown goatee and eyeglasses. The woman had shoulder-length brown hair, a kind face, and was wearing a summer-dress. They had an artistic vibe. That's what they looked like. And sitting there with the woman after the man went searching, I became a little bit embarrassed, since I'd been doing so much screaming and crying just a few moments before.

"I just— I didn't know if I would ever see my family again," I told her.

"Aw, don't worry. I can imagine that'd be very scary. But we'll find her. We will," she said.

I started crying again, and then I stopped. I had so much going through my mind.

"Why would she leave without telling me? What was she thinking?"

The woman sat there a moment, then replied, "She was looking for you when we saw her. She was probably worried. Were you gone a while?"

"Yeah... But still."

As we sat there for some minutes, she made small talk with me, and when she started texting with her husband and I saw that *she* had a cell phone, it occurred to me that I could probably borrow it to call 9-11 (I did not know either of my parents' cell numbers) if we were unable to find my mom, and I felt one thousand times more at ease, like I was back on Earth after a shaky trip to Mars. And then the man with the goatee that'd gone searching for my mom appeared at the other side of the park, walking our way. He was with the park security guard, a tall bald man from either Haiti or Jamaica who was always wearing sunglasses every time we went to that park.

They arrived at the blanket and the security man asked me my name. I told him a false name (Garrett) because even though he was a security guard, I was in the presence of strangers (and I didn't like my name). He asked if I was looking for my mother and I told him yeah. He pulled a slip of paper from his pocket, removed his cell phone from its holster on his belt, pressed some buttons, and lifted the phone to his ear. The person on the other end picked up and he said his name to the person and then he said that her son was here, and I knew it was my mom that he was talking to, and I knew that I would live. He told her where we were, then he handed me the phone so that I could talk to my mom.

A rush of joy entered me. "Hello?" I said.

I heard her take a deep breath, and then she said, "Okay. Are you all right?"

"Yes. But why'd you leave me?"

"I've been looking for you. I have no idea where you've been. But we'll talk about this in a minute. I'm coming to you so just stay right where you are. Okay?"

"Yes. But, where are you?"

"I'm walking through the parking lot. I'll see you in a second. Can you hand the phone back to the man?"

"How'd you know I'm by a man? Can you see me? Mom, where are you?"

"Okay. Um..." She stopped talking, and then less than a minute later I saw her walking up the hill. I ran to her and we hugged, and I told her that she shouldn't have left, and she didn't reply, and we walked back to the couple and the security guard, and she thanked them all, and then we went back to the parking lot to wait for the cops, because she'd called them.

As we waited, my mom said some stuff about taking the effects of my actions into account, and how I shouldn't have hid like that without telling her. I was surprised at her tone, offended almost, because I'd expected her to just be happy to be reunited with her son.

I asked if I was in trouble.

"If you will not take responsibility for your actions, then you will be. You need to acknowledge your mistakes, so that I know you won't make them again."

"Okay..." I said. "But what did I do wrong?"

She thought about it. "If we're out somewhere, you need to tell me if you are going to leave my sight... That's all. It's that simple really."

"Mom, I did tell you. I told you I was going to go see my friends."

"You must realize that seeing your group of friends and hiding out of everyone's sight for thirty minutes are two completely different things."

"How?"

"Don't do this, or you will be in trouble."

"Why are we standing right here?"

"We're going to stand here until the officers arrive. And I need you to acknowledge that you can see the difference between hiding— or, that you can see the importance of letting me know *where* you are."

"Yes. I see the importance of that. I do... But Mom, it's no one's fault. I was looking for you too... So I will tell you where I am, but maybe you can too, because I didn't know where you were when I came back to our spot."

She sighed, and then she said, "Okay."

When the police car got there I explained everything to the two officers and they gave me a lecture about how I shouldn't go hiding without telling people, but I didn't mind because the guy that did all the talking was pretty nice about it. They let me ask some questions about their car and then my mom said we'd already used up enough of their time, and we went home.

She still had me do my homework when we got back, since I'd promised that I would (and I remember I told her that promises can be voided in certain situations, but she disregarded that as child-talk), and the next day after I turned it in, my peers didn't really have much to say about my hiding job.

There are two lessons that can be taken from this story.

1. Do not freak out. Have hope, know that it will be all right, and push through the fright. For a moment I was quite sure that I was doomed, and I almost let my panic engulf me completely. But something inside me told me not to give up, and so I rose to my feet and yelled out, which led me to meet the couple on the blanket, and within ten or fifteen minutes of thinking my mom was gone, and my body panicking and telling me that death was imminent, I was re-united with my mother.

2. If under the age of 18, tell your parents before you go out of their sight for extended periods of time. (If over 18, in my opinion, it is still a good idea to tell people what your plans are. 127 Hours is a perfect example of a man who didn't inform people of his whereabouts, and experienced extreme traumas because of it).

Dax Flame was born in the USA in 1991.

Diary Entry 5/16/12

I found out there are a two movies I can maybe be in. And also tomorrow I am going to audition for a commercial. I think it would be fun to be in a commercial. In one of the movies, the script says I would kiss Jennifer Aniston, and in the other I would play a zombie. Guess which one is preferable...

Yesterday I wrote a little educational fiction story about 'Henry and his Money Dummy', and I also went grocery shopping at Whole Foods. Today I was going to make a smoothie for lunch, I got the frozen fruit out (blueberries, papaya, mango, pineapple), loaded them into the blender, then opened the fridge and realized that once again I had forgotten to get the coconut water. I was pretty amazed at my absent-mindedness, since I'd committed that same error a week or two ago. Why do I always forget stuff (when I shop)? I just sat there staring into the fridge. I cupped my face in my hands. I was pretty disappointed, because I had been anticipating the smoothie, and was also very hungry. With my face in my hands, I took a deep breath, and said to myself, "You moron." then I shut the fridge.

So I had soup and decided I would go to Barnsdall Park, read, and go to Trader Joe's on the way home. While at the park I didn't do much reading. I wasn't really in the mood for some reason. I mostly just did some thinking; about science, about nature, about the two movies, and about my dream from last night. So I was mostly just thinking while I was there. At one point, I was sitting on the side of the hill, in the grass, and some 60-year-old woman with bleached blonde hair and a plastic-surgery alien face (I know that sounds rude, but I'm really not trying to be, it's just a good description of what her face looked like), came huffing and puffing as she walked up the hill. I was watching her. It seemed like a struggle for her. Then she stopped walking, turned to me, and asked, "Do you know where the office is?" I figured she was talking about the building with the art gallery in it, because I've seen an office in it many times when I've gone in to get water or use the bathroom. I smiled friendlily, pointed to the building, and said, "It's right in there." "How do I get up there?" She asked. "You just walk around here, and then up over there." (this doesn't sound like much since I can't type my

33

hand movements, but I was pointing out the way as I said this) "Over the fence?" "Yeah, right behind there." "I have to walk higher?" "Yeah, right to there." She looked down and mumbled something about how hard it was to get wherever she was going, or how much walking she'd done. Then she asked, "Do you know where the studio is?" She seemed to me like maybe she was halfway senile. But maybe not, maybe she was just off. I told her, "I'm not sure..." She didn't respond. I wanted to help her, so I said, "There's an art gallery in that building, and then there's some school on the other side with classrooms I think." The lady didn't say anything, just stood there. A car passed behind her, then she looked at me and said, "What?" (P.S. We were standing like 20 yards from each other. She was lower on the hill than me.) I just repeated exactly what I'd just said. She asked again how to get there, and I pointed out the building again. "And I just walk where?" She asked, and I pointed out the staircase. She began to walk over to it. Her body didn't look so bad or anything, so I wonder why she seemed so out of shape and why walking was so hard for her. As she was walking up the stairs, she said to me accusingly, "You said it was up on the right." I just looked at her, unsure what she was talking about, because I'd said no such thing. Then she said, kind of angrily, "Do you *know* where the office is?" I had an idea that it might be in the building, but I didn't really *know*. So I said, "No, I guess, I don't know." "Then why are you giving me directions?" She asked rheotorically as she shook her head. I thought that was really rude. I was just trying to help her out. I didn't understand why she'd be like that. But I didn't have any urge to confront her or anything, because I mostly felt bad for her. I know when she was a little girl she wouldn't be bitter like that, so I wondered what made her act rude in such a way. Maybe her man left her or she had a disease. I don't know. I saw her ask a couple the same questions as she got to the top of the stairs. The guy answered, and he said about the same thing as me. The lady said something that made the girl of the couple laugh. Why did she charm them, but act rude to me? Still, I hope she found her way all right. (Maybe she was an angel...?)
(Also, I noticed one lady looking at me when I was sitting in a kind of nice position on the hill. She was walking her dog, and she tried to look at me out of the corner of her eye, but I noticed.)

Anyways, I read a tiny bit, but as I mentioned, my mind wasn't in the mood to read today, so I left the park and went to Trader Joe's.

As I walked into the store, I was walking behind a bald man, and his head was right at my eye level. I don't know what I thought of that, but it just stuck out to me for some reason. I got my groceries (Two of which were bottles of coconut water. Thank you.)

The checkout girl didn't talk with me too much, which was a shame. (She had a tattoo.) I took the metro home, and I made a smoothie and drank it while I listened to Golden Oldies, and now I am typing this.

P.S...... I wrote this diary 8 hours ago. It is 6:28AM, so technically it is now 5/17/12, but for some reason I couldn't sleep tonight/last night, so I am writing this on this on this diary entry. I don't know why I didn't sleep. My body or my mind just didn't seem to want to. It's the second time this week. Never does that happen to me. Maybe that's the price you have to pay to have good book ideas? I don't think so. I think I will take a break from writing for a few days. Maybe some lesson will come out of this.

Advertisement:

---

# *Once in a lifetime opportunity!*

This is your chance to enter a living, breathing, *fantasy* world.

Walk on the moon. Swim in lakes of juice. Fly without machines.

All you have to do is step into our machine, which will teleport you to this land of never ending *happiness*...

Disclaimer: Once you go, you may not return. You must go alone.

---

If you saw this ad in the newspaper, would you respond? What if a well-respected doctor vouched his support?

Your answer has the potential to say a lot about you.

If you said yes, it means you are of an escapist attitude. Saying no shows great courage.

## My Brazilian Rome

*A tale of love in the city of love.*


The train rolled down the tracks and pulled to a stop at Roma Termini shortly after the sun had set. I stepped out into the evening, took the map that I'd printed up back in the U.S. from my back pocket, and used it to find my way to the Mosaic Hostel. A soft-spoken, blonde-haired lady around twenty-nine checked me in, gave me a tourist map, and then showed me to my dorm. The train ride from La Spezia had been a crowded one and I was quite tired, so after unpacking my bags I decided I'd stay in for the night and go about exploring Rome tomorrow.

Before lying down, I sat on my bed for a little while and loosely planned out the next four days. There were a few sights that I knew I wanted to see, and the tourist map the receptionist had given me had all the popular attractions highlighted. As I was doing a little research on my laptop, a young woman with brunette hair entered the room and we said hello. She was from Australia, and was sleeping in the bunk below mine. The two beds of the other bunk in the room were unoccupied. I returned to my planning, and when my plans were set I went to sleep.

I woke up the next morning to the sound of traffic coming from the street below. Mellow sunbeams slid in through the curtains, and I was feeling good. I looked over the side of my bunk and immediately noticed that a dark-haired girl was sleeping in one of the beds of the bunk that had been unoccupied the night before. I assumed she must've gotten in pretty late. The Australian woman was already up and gone. I changed out of my pajamas and went downstairs to get some food. I was pretty starved, and was slightly disappointed to find that the complimentary breakfast was cereal and Pop-Tart-like breakfast bars. I skipped the complimentary breakfast, left the hostel, ate a few bananas from a nearby convenience store, then opened the tourist map and set out to begin my first day of exploring.

First I went to the Trevi Fountain, which the blond-haired lady had recommended highly. I didn't have too much trouble finding it and had a fine walk there. It was a very pretty fountain, and about one or two

37

thousand people were gathered around it taking pictures and throwing coins at it. I looked at it a bit, snapped a few photos, and then began walking to the Coliseum. There were a few ruins along the way, and I took photos of these as well. They didn't really look like much—just like some tumpled over buildings—until I used my imagination. When I did use my imagination, they were pretty amazing. I didn't know much about the history, but I did know that Rome was once the heart of civilization, an ancient metropolis. I imagined the Czars and the Cesars walking on the same land that I was walking on, carrying their scrolls, thousands of years earlier... "What would they think if they could see me now?" "How did their city fall?" "*Why* is it in ruins?" It was interesting to think about. I walked on and arrived at the Coliseum, which was surrounded by many more ruins. I didn't go inside, but I stood and absorbed its grandeur from the outside. It was amazing to think about too. I had not seen Gladiator at that point, but I knew a little about what had gone on in there—the gladiators and such.

I ate lunch and walked around a while longer, exploring a few of Rome's parks and neighborhoods. Day gave way to dusk, and I began back towards the hostel. Maybe I would see the Vatican and Sistine Chapel tomorrow.

I said hello to the blonde-haired lady as I made my way through the lobby and up the stairs to my dorm. As I entered the room, I saw that the only person there was the dark-haired girl who I'd seen sleeping in the previously unoccupied bed that morning. She was sitting on her bed reading a book. We made eye contact but did not say anything. She was pretty, with a Latin complexion and straight black hair. I climbed onto my bunk, opened my diary, and began to write as much as I could remember about my day—events, thoughts, etc. After I finished scribbling everything down I was ready to get some food, but felt like staying in the room with the girl a bit longer. So I continued to sit, and I moved my pencil a centimeter above the page, pretending to write more as I stole occasional glances at her. I noticed that her book was Eat Pray Love.

"How is that book?" I asked, setting the pencil down.

"I just started it. I like it," she replied in an accent I could not place my finger on.

"Oh. Have you seen the movie?"

She put the book on her knee and said, "Yes, it's very good. It's what made me want to read the book. It's about love." She laughed.

"Where are you from?"

"I am from Brazil. And you?"

"The U.S."

"Oh. How long are you in Rome?"

"Four more nights."

"Oh lucky! I am here for only two more nights. Are you travelling through Europe, or just in Rome?"

I told her about my trip and asked about hers. She had just come in from Barcelona—where she had spent a week and a half—and was heading back to Brazil after her two days in Rome. I told her my name and asked hers.

"I am Pamela."

"Oh. Pamela."

"Yes... What are you doing anyways?" she asked as she stood up and approached me to take a look at my notebook. I shut it before she could see anything, and told her I was just planning my trip. She thought I was joking I suppose, because she laughed, and then sat back down.

"I'm hungry," she said.

I didn't know what to say, so I said nothing. She looked around the room.

"I'm hungry," she said again.

"What are you going to eat?"

"Are you hungry?" she asked me.

"Yes. I am."

"Me too."

She stared at me. I thought I could sense something.

"Do you want to get something to eat?" I asked.

"Yes. Let's do that." She put her book on the bed and stood up. I was pretty thrilled, but acted cool. I hopped off the bed, threw on my sweater, and asked, "What would you like?" She told me about a pizza place she'd gone to for lunch earlier in the day. I said it sounded good and together we left. As we walked down the street she told me about

39

her life in Brazil. She'd majored in linguistics, and was now working at a hotel in Rio. She loved the job, even though the hours were pretty tough. I asked if she ever wanted to move to America. She thought for a moment, and then said yes, but that it is very difficult to become a citizen. "Can you get a green card if you get married?" I asked. She told me that that would work too, and I couldn't help but smile.

We arrived at the pizza place. It really wasn't that impressive to me, just a typical fast-food pizza place, but I pretended to be impressed for her. I didn't even ask her to, but she bought my pizza for me. She was embarrassed that she'd gotten two more pieces than I had, but I told her, "Don't be. I just hate pizza," which was a mistake. It kind of hurt her feelings because she thought she'd brought me to some great place. But she wasn't too touchy about it or anything, and we just kept on talking. I asked a lot of questions about Brazil. Any time I tried to be funny, she laughed pretty good. By the time we'd finished our food and had begun walking back, we'd kind of run out of general introductory things to talk about, and we walked down the sidewalk in silence. I looked at her, unsure if she was still interested in me. I wondered if I should reach out to hold her hand, but I didn't.

I said, "I like your boots."

"Thank you," she replied with a fantastic smile.

And then she started a conversation about frozen yogurt. I didn't have much to contribute, but I didn't mind listening.

When we arrived back at the hostel, Pamela told me about a walking tour she was planning to take the next day, and invited me to come. I accepted immediately. Upstairs in our room, the Australian woman and a new girl were asleep in their beds. I changed into my pajamas and Pamela did the same, and before going to bed she told me she'd wake me up in the morning at nine forty-five. I said all right, we told each other goodnight, and went to sleep.

I woke up around nine thirty the next morning to the sound of Pamela speaking. She was speaking with another girl. I sat up and looked over the side of my bunk to see who exactly the second voice belonged to, and saw that Pamela was speaking not with the Australian woman, but with the other girl that we'd seen sleeping in the dorm's fourth bed the night before. They were speaking in a foreign language that I soon learned to be Portuguese. I said good morning and Pamela said hi and told me that this girl was also from Brazil—from Sao Paulo—her name was Cristina, and that she'd invited her to join us on the walking tour. To be honest, I thought that having a third person on the tour might make things a bit less romantic, but I didn't say so because really I didn't mind. I got dressed, and the three of us went downstairs for breakfast. They loved the cereal and Pop-Tart things and begged me to try them, but I wouldn't. Pamela teased me about it, but when I asked her to stop teasing me, she stopped. After they finished eating, we left the hostel, picked up a few bananas for my breakfast, and then headed towards the tour's starting point a few blocks away.

We arrived a little bit early, so we just talked as we waited. The more we talked, the more I came to admire Pamela. Occasionally her and Cristina would begin speaking in Portuguese, but then they'd remember I couldn't understand them and would go back to English. Cristina's English was very poor, whereas Pamela's was excellent. They liked my jokes. Slowly others began to arrive for the tour, and then the tour-guide—a short, young Italian lady who, I believe, had a doctorate in Roman history (she also spoke about doing some archeology)— arrived and the tour began.

It was a good tour. Pamela was more focused on learning than I was. I attempted to show my interest by answering a few of the guide's questions during the tour, but failed each time. It was kind of a phony thing to try and do, but it didn't seem to do any harm, Pamela didn't seem any less interested in me.

After we finished the tour, we tipped the guide and went out for lunch. We ate at a very pretty outdoor alleyway café. The waiter brought us bread and Pamela and Cristina ordered wine. I didn't order any, but he brought us back three glasses anyway. The Italian waiter flirted with Cristina by complimenting her eyes, which truthfully were quite alluring. I wondered if I should stand up and tell him to ease it, but she seemed to be flattered by it. I ordered a salad, Pamela ordered pasta, and Cristina ordered steak. The food was delicious. We all talked. They liked my jokes. Pamela offered me some of her pasta and I said no thanks, which seemed to disappoint her. I apologized and told her I hated pasta. She told me that I didn't eat enough. Cristina agreed. I just smiled at Pamela, and then I decided to step out of my comfort zone. "Give me your pasta," I told her. She laughed and handed it to me. I began to eat it. I've never been a fan of pasta with white sauce on it, but I ate it anyway. They laughed as they watched me. I really did not enjoy the food, but I enjoyed their laughter. I kept eating it and kept eating it, but then Pamela said, "Okay, okay! Don't eat it all," and took the bowl back from me. But I felt that it might have helped to prove that I was highly interested in her.

Whenever Cristina spoke English, she spoke really slow, and had to think for a while after you said something to her. She was very pretty, and it made her appear ditzy. Of course, I'd probably have looked stupider than a baby if I tried to speak Portuguese. At one point I noticed she was staring at me, and then she said, "Your eyes are beautiful." I could tell she was just being nice and not hitting on me, and I was flattered, but I didn't want Pamela to think I cared what Cristina thought, so I told Cristina, "Why don't you stop staring at me and eat your steak." It was pretty rude, I hadn't intended to be so harsh, but I think the rudeness was lost in translation, because she just smiled and took a drink of her wine. I looked at Pamela, but couldn't tell whether she was satisfied by my response or not.

They ordered tiramisu for desert, and didn't talk at all but just said "Mmmm," over and over as they ate it. Cristina offered me some of hers and I said no thanks. Then Pamela offered me some of hers, and I didn't want to say no, so I accepted the spoonful and slyly spit it into my napkin so that they couldn't tell. She asked what I thought and I told her it was delicious. She offered me another bite and I said no thanks. She insisted, so I accepted it and then spit it into the napkin. We did this two more times, she never noticed my trick, and then she finished it.

After lunch they wanted to see the Trevi fountain, so I went with them and saw it again. They thought it was the most magnificent thing in the world. As I watched Pamela marvel at the statues in the fountain, I imagined us traveling the world together. In a way, I thought, we already were. She looked over at me and I smiled at her. She smiled back and asked me to take her picture. She handed me the camera, posed, smiled, and I took it.

"That's a beautiful picture," I told her.

She smiled and seemed genuinely flattered when I said that. She didn't seem to even be able to think of what to say, so she turned and asked Cristina to take a picture of us. We stood next to each other, she put her arm around me, I put mine around her, and Cristina took the photo.

We left the Trevi fountain after a while and walked on to the Pantheon. I got a banana from a food cart on the way, and Cristina called me monkey boy. I didn't laugh and she told me she was only joking. I wondered how she could not know she was being offensive. We got to the Pantheon and went inside. Something about that building was pretty awesome—almost beyond comprehension. It's about three or four thousand years old, and it has a big hole in the ceiling that the sun shines through to create a circle of light on the ground. If you watch the circle long enough, you can see it moving *very* slowly, and it's kind of like watching the Earth rotate.

After the Pantheon we headed to our last stop of the day, the building called the Vittoriano. It was fantastic looking. Fantastic. Flags, guards, statues jutting up into the sky. We went up to the second story to stand on the roof part. It was great. Cristina said she was going to take an elevator ride to the very top, but me and Pamela stayed back because the line for the elevator was too long. It worked out perfectly because it allowed us some time alone. We walked over to the edge of the building and looked out across the rustic Roman rooftops. Then we witnessed an amazing sight. As the sun set, an eternal river of birds began flowing through the sky. Thousands and thousands, for minutes and minutes, just flowed across the purple and orange evening sky. I looked at Pamela, she looked out across the city, the breeze blew gently, and something told me to take hold of her hand. I reached out, and did it. She smiled and held mine back. Together we stood, holding hands, enjoying the beautiful view...

That was my favorite part about Rome.

After Vittoriano, we took the Metro back to our hostel. On the way, we were discussing the Coliseum, and I mentioned that I hadn't seen the movie Gladiator. They were shocked, and we decided that if the hostel had it, we'd watch it when we got back. At the hostel, the blonde-haired lady informed us that they did indeed have it. We celebrated, borrowed it, ran to our room, changed into pajamas, sat in a row on the Pamela's bunk bed, and I put the DVD into my laptop. Since I was sitting in the middle, the laptop was on my lap. The movie was magnificent. Pamela was sitting very close to me, and about halfway through the movie, she rested her head on my shoulder, just for a moment. After it was finished, Pamela told me something about how she'd seen on the History channel that they used to fill the coliseum with water and have boat battles in it. I didn't think that sounded very plausible, but I let it slide. We were both kind of sad as we said good night, because Pamela would be leaving the next morning at eleven. But we said goodnight, and fell asleep.

In the morning I gave Pamela a hug and we began our goodbye. I wondered if it would be weird if I told her I loved her. I felt kind of like I really did. She didn't seem to want to go. I decided against saying it, but when she went to check out, I took out my diary, ripped out a blank piece of paper, and quickly drew a rough sketch of her face and wrote below it, *I love you Pamela. Thank you.* and slipped it into her purse. After that, she came back up to get her bags, we said our final goodbye, and then she left. It made me a little sad that she wasn't going to be around with me that day, but I counted my blessings instead of sheep. I went to the Vatican, and although I did not see the Pope, I did see the Sistine Chapel. My god, it was incredible... They had this long hallway with paintings just lining the ceiling, and tiles intricately placed all over the ground. I felt like a sardine in a can since there were so many people there, but I didn't mind.

Cristina and me had arranged to meet up at the hostel so we could have dinner together. We went and grabbed Ethiopian food across the street from the hostel. It was really great food. You had to eat it with your hands, which was unique. I enjoyed eating with Cristina and reflecting on the time we'd spent with Pamela. I asked her if she thought Pamela loved me. She said that Pamela did love me. I don't think she really understood what I was talking about, but I just pretended she did, and that was enough for me.

Excerpt from Diary Entry 5/15/12: ... *Then after I finished that at 3:30AM, I laid in bed, but I couldn't sleep because I was having so many cool book ideas. One of those ideas is why YOU are reading this right now (whoever you are). It was the idea that my diary entries will be included in the book too. So that the readers can see what process is like for me to write the book. It would be almost like including a tutorial of how to write one. I'm just going to write the diaries regular though, I'm not going to include lessons in them, that's what the stories are for. I'll include some of my diaries from my past too.*

*And then, another idea that was keeping me up that I was excited about is this. I can include web addresses to exclusive videos in the book. Oh my gosh. That way, only the people who have the book can watch the videos.*
...

Excerpt from Diary Entry 5/18/12: ... *Today my friend, who I wanted to help me make an exclusive video for my book, got the e-mail that I'd sent him the other day, and said "yes," he wants to shoot a video this weekend. This is excellent. I think it will be about photography, as that is something I really have gotten into and developed an eye for during my travels. So at least one good thing came out of that commercial audition. The idea for this video. ...*

Excerpt from Diary Entry 5/20/12: ... *Then, I spent the evening shooting the Photography video. It was a success. ...*

Diary Entry 5/23/12: *So we filmed the second part of the video today. I went and took pictures of people. It went astonishingly. I got some nice pics. Humans, nature, cars, architecture. Very nice pics. Interesting and fun.*

Excerpt from Diary Entry 6/9/12: *I have not been writing any self-help stories lately because I have been writing the words/voiceovers/lessons for the photography video. I am just now finishing with it. It is a handsome success. ...*

That is Andy DeYoung.

I took this picture of him near the Observatory in Griffith Park.

He is filming me with that camera of his right there.

To see the footage he filmed of me as I took this photo (and many more), follow this exclusive link:

http://www.youtube.com/watch?v=ffce934_zU8

(Proceed through the following pages after viewing the video)

I hope you enjoyed the video, and that you possibly even learned a thing or two about a hobby I care earnestly about. I took 137 photos during our two-day shoot; here are a few of my favorites:

Title: **Berries Rosaceous**

Notes: Excellent contrast (as mentioned in the video).

Title: **Just One**

Notes: Great use of color (thin blue leash) and shadow. I really like this one.

Title: **You Can't Grab a Shadow**

Note: Interesting composition and possible conceptual abilities.

Title: **Observatory Jagged**

Notes: Excellent use of lines and composition. I think it's the most striking or bold.

Title: **Touch the Wind**

Notes: Natural and interesting, with pure/tranquil aura.

Title: **Hollywood Lovers**                    (*Blurred faces for privacy)

Notes: A *true* <u>portrait</u> of two young hearts in full tilt. Radiating their nuance as I set up and take my photo. In my opinion, the choice shot of the lot.

[Note: I wrote thirteen short stories in April 2012, and twelve in May.]

# Sweet Vengeance

During the summer of '06 I spent a week at my cousin's house while my parents were at sea. On my second day there my cousin punched me in the face when he realized that I'd eaten the rest of his ice cream when he'd left to use the bathroom in the middle of watching E.T. At fourteen I was a year older than him, but his muscles had developed prematurely and the blow had almost knocked me unconscious, so instead of striking him back I cried out to his mother, my aunt, who appeared at the top of the staircase, asking what was wrong. After I told her, she sent my cousin to his room to think about what he'd done and gave me a bag of ice to hold on my cheek while I watched the rest of the movie.

After E.T. was over, I had some chicken at the dining room table with my aunt, uncle, and cousin. My aunt mentioned what'd happened and my uncle told us he didn't want us doing any more fighting. My cousin and I didn't speak a word to each other throughout the dinner, and each time we exchanged glances I saw malice in his eyes. I knew he wasn't happy that I'd told on him, and I certainly didn't feel that being sent to his room had been punishment enough, so I knew that it was going to be a violent week.

That night, for protection, I got a metal baseball bat from their garage, took it upstairs, and slid it into my sleeping bag. I wanted it by my side if my cousin tried to attack me while I was asleep. But the night went by without attack, and, because my cousin spent most of his time that week at his friend's house, so did the next three days. Each of those three nights when he was back from his friend's for dinner, I'd look across the table at him to see if I could detect any remaining malice in his face, and gradually, night-by-night, it seemed to go away. And on the sixth night I could see none of it. There were only two nights remaining in my stay and that punch had been the only violence to occur. My cousin and I even spoke a few pleasant words to each other as we ate. It seemed to me that my prediction of violence had been mistaken, and my sleeping with the bat for not. And then, as we were washing the dishes after dinner, my aunt informed us that that afternoon she'd rented a movie and purchased ice cream. My cousin's eyes met mine. I didn't know what he was thinking, but at the words 'ice cream' I sensed that the peace would be shaken.

My aunt said we could help ourselves to the desert when we were finished cleaning, and as soon as the last dish was put away, my cousin raced to the freezer and I followed right behind. It was a half-gallon carton of Dutch chocolate, and he took it out and held it under his arm as he went to get himself a bowl and spoon. He served a couple scoops into his bowl, and as I looked on I couldn't help but feel that I should do something to earn that punch to the face he'd given me a few days before. But I also knew that if I tried to do anything to his ice cream at that moment, he'd hit me again, and if I tried to sneak up and smash my bowl into his head or something along those lines, his mom would hear and I'd be dead. Plus, that type of action seemed like too much at the time—all I wanted to do was something to ruin his ice cream eating experience.

When the bowl was full, he put the lid on the carton and looked at me. I looked back. I tried not to be the first to break eye contact, but I was. He smiled and put the ice cream in the freezer. It felt like I was once again being slapped in the face, because he could have just handed the carton to me. He walked into the living room, took a seat on the couch, and I went about fixing my bowl, not a pleasant thought in my head.

I took a seat with my bowl of ice cream in my hands at the far end of the couch. We each ate a couple bites, looking up at the blank T.V. screen. My aunt had put the DVD in the player, but she was no longer in the room, so one of us would have to start it.

"Go press play. You're closer," my cousin told me.

"Don't tell me what to do," I said.

"You're closest, and you should have already done it because you sat down last."

"If you try and boss me around, or anything, one more ti—"

"What? You'll tell my mom?" He laughed.

Gripping my bowl tight in my left hand, I leaned across the couch and tried to swat his bowl out of his hands with my right. But he was ready for it, and moved his bowl quickly out of the way. My hand hit nothing but air, and, looking at my legs, his eyes went wide, and he laughed, "Nice move!"

On the couch, floor, and my pants was chocolate ice cream. I'd tilted my bowl when I'd swung for his. Anger started to bubble, and I simply wanted to destroy him. But if I attacked now, he'd be expecting it and I'd stand no chance. He could see the anger, and laughed more. I put my bowl on the coffee table and started towards the stairs.

"Where are you going? You can't just leave this mess? I'll tell my mom!" He was laughing so hard I thought he might cry.

Upstairs in the game-room I pulled the bat from my sleeping bag. Without even hiding it behind my back I walked right downstairs, through the living room (ignoring my cousin's questions), and into their garage.

There, to the left of the door, was his scooter—electric, red, beautiful. Supposedly it went fifteen miles-per-hour, but I couldn't say for sure, because I'd never once been allowed to ride it.

My first swing cracked the rearview mirror that rose from the left handlebar. A swing, a swing, and a swing later the mirror was in pieces, scattered across the ground. Next my eyes were drawn to the speedometer. Whack, crack, *pshew*. Smashed it in with a single swing, and then two more to be sure.

"Oh my *God*!"

My cousin was standing in the doorway. My breathing was heavy and my mind was buzzing. He came towards me but I waved the bat back and forth in front of me so he couldn't get close enough to do anything. Looking again at his scooter, he shouted, "What *the*...? You're freaking insane!"

I just waited, with the bat ready. He turned to his dad's tool-chest, grabbed a handful of screws, and just as he was about to throw them at me, his mom appeared in the doorway behind him, grabbed his arm, and put an immediate end to our tussle.

But, she was too late. I had already won the war, and there was one useless speedometer and one thousand shards of scattered glass to prove it.

Neither of us was allowed to watch the movie that night, and my parents lectured me and grounded me after returning from their trip and hearing of my destruction. But I didn't feel one twinge of regret. I'd shown my cousin who the boss of me was. Me.

What lesson can be taken from this?
Sometimes we must be creative when sticking up for ourselves. When you cannot destroy the person, destroy or do something else. Sticking up for yourself improves self-esteem, and proves to the enemy that you are not a punching bag.

True Fact: My cousin once had to get rabies vaccinations.

I'm someone who likes fighting. I like to fight, and I like punching people. That said, I do realize that if we could eliminate violence from humankind, it would be for the greater good of the world and those living in it. But until that has been accomplished, fighting is sometimes unavoidably *necessary*.

As a pretty inactive junior in high school, I was always looking for something to do, so when my mom asked me if I could drive to the gas station to fill up her tank one spring afternoon, I obliged her with gratitude. She handed me the keys and I drove to the station, parked at a pump, locked the door, and went in to pay for the gas and to get myself a drink. I got a juice, headed for the register, and spotted a glass case containing many daggers and a few swords. Not bad. I approached it and let my eyes survey the silver weapons. I'll have the have the samurai please. The gas employee came over, unlocked the case, and gave me the dagger. I paid for $40 of gas, $4 of juice, and $29 of metal weaponry.

I drank down the juice as the gas flowed into the tank. The bottle was empty just as the tank was full. I tossed the juice, racked the pump, and ignited the ignition. I drove to the chicken drive-through next door and placed an order for a half-dozen rolls. I gave this order frequently and had the exact change in cash. I'd be paying with my own money since my mom had only given permission to use her card to purchase things from the gas station. As I pulled towards the window a young lady came out and delivered my bagged rolls, since it was a simple order and the car in front of me might be at the window a bit longer. I gave her the exact change and was good to go. I put the car in reverse, rolled up my window, and backed up, into a truck, who's driver yelled, "What the f*ck are you doing?!"

I looked into the rearview mirror and realized. I have no words for the fear—or the... doom—that I felt. The man's face was bearded and he wore sunglasses. As he stepped out of the silver truck I observed his physique, which was grandiose. I put my mom's car in park. I closed my eyes. I took two deep breaths, and then opened my door.

The man was bent over looking at his bumper. I took the opportunity to look back into my mom's car to see where the dagger was—on the passengers seat.

I waited, to see what he would say first. If he said something that signified that he would try to kill me, I'd jump into the car and lock the door; and then, if he broke the window, only then, I'd put the dagger to use.

"Mine is fine," he said calmly, referring to the bumper.

I approached with caution. The tone he'd spoken with put me much more at ease, but you never know. I glanced at the bumpers.

"Yours has those little dents. Mine's fine."

I looked at him. This was a different man than the one that yelled the F-word moments before. This man would not do me any harm. There would be no need for violence. I apologized and we parted ways.

But what if those two little dents had been on his bumper, and not my mom's? Then he'd have been that same angry man who'd screamed the curse word. He'd be that man so drunk with anger that the animal inside him takes over and he tries everything he can to beat me down into the pulp that this rage makes him feel I deserve to become. And that is when I fight back. That is when I punch the throat, and kick out his knees, and even slice his shoulder if he does not relent. Please notice that these techniques are only done to disarm him from attacking me—they are self-defense techniques, not offensive.

And before sharing my concluding sentence, I must note that violence can also most certainly be unnecessary. Most certainly. More often than not. Yes, throwing a pointless punch can be fun in its inexplicable way—that's what makes people do it. And other times throwing one can make you sick to the stomach. As a freshman I accidently assaulted an authority figure in the crotch as a joke; the punch felt terrible—seeing him drop in pain—but the laughs of the class were glorious. It was an indulgent and unnecessary punch. So I agree that *this* type of violence is wrong.

But two simple dents were what separated me from fighting and not fighting that man. And so, in this world, where anything can happen, fighting can be necessary.

# Broken

*Commend, don't condemn.*

With my left hand I lifted the wooden pencil and inserted the tip as far as it could go into the silver sharpener. Then, because my right arm was in a sling, I let go of the pencil, moved my left hand to the handle of the sharpener, and began to crank it. With nothing to hold the pencil in place, it rotated unsharpened at the same pace as the handle. I leaned my face forward and tried to hold the pencil steady with my teeth. I cranked the handle a few times and could feel the pencil being sharpened, but the method was far too awkward and inefficient to carry on with. I relaxed my jaws—releasing the pencil from my teeth—stood upright, resisted the urge to smack my hand against the whiteboard, and sighed.

"Do you need any help?" asked Mr. Keyes, the middle-aged Physics teacher, sitting behind his desk.

"Yes. *Please.*"

"Okay. James, would you mind helping him?"

James, who sat near the whiteboard at the front of his row, stood from his desk and approached me and the sharpener.

"I'll twist it if you hold the pencil," I suggested.

"I can just do it."

"Um..."

He placed one hand on the pencil and the other on the crank.

"Stop..." I said.

He looked at me.

"I want to sharpen it actually," I told him.

"Okay..."

He eyed me for a few seconds, walked back to his desk, and resumed his test. Mr. Keyes was watching me, but Mr. Keyes had a small body and a quiet manner, so I wasn't afraid.

I turned back to the sharpener and wrapped the fingers of my left hand around the pencil, my right arm dangling limp in its sling. I contemplated one-handed sharpening methods. I moved quite close to the sharpener, bent down, and leaned my chest against it so that my left shoulder could hold the pencil in place. But I could barely crank the handle with my left hand from this angle.

I took a step back, and with my right hand still dangling loose, I lifted my arm in its sling and pushed it against the pencil. I then reached across my right arm with my left, grabbed the handle, and cranked.

It was an effective method. I cranked a few more times, letting out a quiet little, "Ouch…" with each rotation.

There was a tap on my shoulder and I turned to find the blonde-haired Mr. Keyes standing behind me.

"Can I help you with your pencil?"

"I think I've already pretty much sharpened it."

"Okay, well… I don't want you to hurt your arm…"

A few students were looking up at me from their tests.

"Yeah. My wrist is broken, and my collarbone is broken, so… But, um, I didn't want to distract James from his test."

"All right. Well, would you mind if I finish sharpening it for you?"

"Yeah, that would be really nice."

He removed the pencil from the sharpener, checked the tip to see how much it needed sharpened, put it back in, and then started cranking.

As he did so, I glanced around the classroom to see who had heard what I'd said about my arm. The few that had looked up were now back to working on their tests.

"Here you go."

Mr. Keyes handed me the pencil and I started back up the aisle towards my desk. He followed behind me, heading towards his desk in the back of the classroom.

"I broke my arm—well, my wrist—and my collarbone last night…" I said, looking over my shoulder at him.

Mr. Keyes nodded with a sympathetic frown on his lips.

"From a car accident."

"Okay. Well maybe you can tell me after class… All right?" he whispered.

"Okay." Then, as I took a seat at my desk and he passed by, I added, "A car ran into me on my scooter."

He nodded, walked on, and before turning back to my test I took a glance around to see who had heard. Samantha, who sat one desk in front of me in the row to my left, seemed to have heard, because she was looking over her shoulder at me, and also David, who sat behind me, was looking at me when I turned around and looked at him.

Even though I had been in no such accident and the arm and collarbone were not actually broken, I continued to let out the occasional moan of agony throughout the test. They sometimes drew the attention that I hoped they would, and when they did not I let out either a louder or more prolonged moan.

At the end of class I turned in my test, and when we got our grades back the next week I was not all that surprised to find that I'd scored a 54. I did not care so much either.

I did many things like this in the later half of my junior year. For some reason, I just started to crave more attention during that time. I did some embarrassing things and also some bad things. Mr. Keyes' classroom was one of the easiest to act out in, because Mr. Keyes was a somewhat shy man and was not at all a strict disciplinarian. I once spat on his black slacks as he walked by my desk, and no one but me and a couple other students behind me noticed. Often—well, a few times at least—I'd go up to that very sharpener as Mr. Keyes gave his lessons and I'd sharpen, sharpen, sharpen, and sharpen my pencil until there was nothing left but an eraser. I don't know why I did this. I probably did it because he didn't like to get me in trouble and it got me attention. I was a troubled junior, and my actions were sometimes pretty rude.

But I do not condemn myself for having had a flustered mind. I actually commend myself, because having gone through those times I've emerged on the other side with a knowledge and understanding of what it's like to go through them. The teen years can be very confusing and I do not believe in condemning any teenager for having a flustered mind. There are always confusing times in life, so adults cannot be condemned either. Regardless of their age, it is important to approach flustered people with a sense of understanding. If someone is acting out for attention, maybe they just need to be listened to. Or if someone is trying to share something with you, maybe deep down they are just asking you to teach them something, even if they aren't sure what.

# Trying to Tutor

*A simple lesson on teaching.*

I had to go to tutoring because my Spanish grade was suffering. Mr. Breel was my twenty-six year old teacher with a tall, thin body. I was a junior.

We sat down at a couple of desks together after school, and instead of jumping right into the teaching, Mr. Breel asked how my day was.

"Good," I answered.

He nodded. "How's your year been?"

"Good."

He smiled politely. "What... uh... what's your favorite class?"

"Spanish."

It was not true, but it came to my head so I said it.

"Oh, it is?" His expression did not show if he believed me or didn't. "Well that's good to hear... You seem to be having a hard time lately."

I thought about it.

"Yeah..." I agreed. "I haven't been doing as well."

"Well... is there a reason?"

I looked at his face. He was looking at me quite respectfully. He was not going to just tutor me and send me out the door. I thought about the question.

"Yeah," I answered.

He waited, then asked, "Well, do you mind me asking what that reason is?"

I had to think of a reason.

"I think... I don't know how to follow the lessons."

He considered the answer.

"At the beginning of the year," he said, "you were having less trouble..."

I waited, and watched as he turned his head and looked distantly across the room for a moment, and then back at me.

"I think you're a very smart guy. And... I hope that you are trying as hard as you can."

He stopped to give me a chance to reply, but I didn't, because I knew there was more coming, and wondered where it was going.

"When I was in high school, or in college," he said," I didn't try as hard as I could have. I'm happy with where I am, but if I had tried harder—if someone had been there to tell me to just *try*—I could have done very well."

I nodded understandingly, but really I was figuring out his motives.

"I feel like you can do quite a lot if you try," he said. "You're very smart, man. Very smart."

He leaned back in his chair, his head tilted, and now I knew he was done and ready for my reply.

I looked down at the desk and assessed the situation.

It seemed to me, at the time, like he was jealous of my sense of wonder—something he must've lost years ago.

"You shouldn't worry," I said to him, then looked up. "You shouldn't have regrets."

He searched my eyes for a moment, then replied, "I don't have regrets. I'm happy. I just, uh... I want you to know that you have the opportunity, and the ability, to do whatever you want to do... It's just very important to try."

"What's your favorite color?"

He had not expected the question.

"What?"

"What is your favorite color?"

It'd popped into my head while he was talking, and while it certainly did seem on the surface like a big change of topic, to me it was actually kind of relevant, because such a detail would help me to know Mr. Breel as more of a person than as a plain-teacher.

He laughed a little and asked, "Why are you asking me this?"

"Sorry," I said, "it's just, I think you are a good teacher, and you should be... proud."

"Thank you," he said, sitting more forward in his chair—but it didn't seem to me like he was able to absorb the compliment fully.

"Yeah," I told him. "It's important that you don't spend too much time regretting."

"I can't say I don't agree," he said, and gave a little chuckle. He paused for a moment, the smirk on his lips, thinking, then he folded his arms and said, "But listen man, you've gotta try."

I nodded. "I always try my very best."

"Good," he said with a smile.

He tutored me through my review sheet good, and I got near-perfect score on my re-quiz.

Teaching is a two-way road.

Diary Entry 6/27/12

I have been visiting with family. In all truth, it has been devine. I have a
new development in my life, and I would like to write about it.
So... two weeks ago yesterday, I auditioned with Jason Sudeikis for the
Jennifer Aniston movie. It was a chemistry read. I did a tremendous
job. The director seemed to like me, and so did the actor Jason
Sudeikis. My manager told me I was one of the final four people they
were considering when I called him after the audition. Now, a couple
days ago, I looked at my computer and searched the movie title (which
is We're the Millers) on Google news. I saw that another boy got offered the role, which was a little disappointing, because I was ninety-
percent sure I was going to be in it. He is from Britain. I wish him well,
but part of me is hoping he screws it up. His name is Will Poulter. (But
listen, it is okay. Truly. I am happy and will continue to have a fine time
with my family. I saw my cousin. I still believe I will be in another
movie sometime.)
Also, I re-read and edited 'The Hide and The Seek'. It's now a first-class
story, and the dialogue is the best.
I saw Men in Black 3 with my mother and my 8 year-old cousin. We
really had a ball while watching that movie. Will Smith is, in my opinion, a classic crowd-charmer. He charmed my mom and cousin, that's
for sure. And judging by the sound of the audience's laughter, they
were not alone in this sensation. I enjoyed it too. I gave my cousin a
little black shirt to wear, and he really looked sleek for an 8 year-old.
He told me he has seen 21 Jump Street five times, and because of this,
he looks up to me, and he truly trusts my opinion. He was staying at
our house last week, that's why he went with us.

*Movie idea I had October 2011 while in Cinque Terre, Italy.*

Logline: Two spies on separate missions (Brad Pitt and Tom Cruise) vie for the affection of a charming hotel owner (Keira Knightley). A love triangle forms. What will happen?

Note: I picture this movie to be somewhat of a romantic thriller piece, which has its share of romantic fun, while maintaining an intense mood throughout. Ideally a director such as David Fincher (top choice) or Darren Arnofsky would helm it.

## Love and Death in the Cinque Terre

Brad and Tom are spies on different missions, each searching for someone (though neither know who exactly they're looking for) as they travel separately through the Italian Riviera. Keira owns a hotel in Riamaggiore that both men happen to have rooms reserved at, at the same time. Tom arrives first, and Keira falls for him the second he flashes her a smile. He asks her if she recommends any dinner spots in town, she begins to recommend one, he cuts her off, and says, "Wait... Don't tell me. Just surprise me when we go there *together* tonight." She smiles, he returns it, and they make plans for eight.

Tom goes up to his room, opens his backpack, unloads a fold out machine gun and two pistols, and does some research on his highly advanced laptop. As he does this, we see that Brad has arrived. Keira can't believe her luck, two studs at her hotel in one day. Brad is happy to see Keira as well. Before they even begin to discuss accommodation details, Brad asks her what she's doing tonight. "Well... I've got some plans, but I might be able to meet you around... ten?" She says. Brad agrees, and she shows him to his room. As soon as she closes the door Brad opens his suitcase and reveals an AK-47, a sniper rifle, and two-dozen grenades.

At eight, Tom meets Keira in the lobby. She looks absolutely stunning. Earlier when we saw her working at the hotel desk, she was wearing glasses and sweatpants and a t-shirt, but now her hair and face are made up beautifully, the glasses are gone, and she wears a magnificent white gown that shimmers in the moonlight. "You look... Fan-*tastic*." Tom says. Keira smiles shyly, they lock arms and Keira leads Tom to her favorite restaurant, hand over his eyes so it'll be a surprise, not letting him look at anything until they are seated. She lifts her hand and Tom is at a loss for words. They have an ocean view that is abso- lutely <u>magical</u>, with the full moon and stars reflected on the water's surface. "What do you think?" Keira asks, unsure. Tom brushes her cheek with his thumb and says, "*Exquisite.*"

They enjoy their meal. Tom orders a shrimp soup, and finds that the shrimp are still in the shell, which leads to many laughs between the two as he tries to figure out how to eat them. Mid-way through the meal Tom's sunglasses start vibrating, and he excuses himself to the bathroom for a moment. Once inside, he presses a button on the glasses and a deep grizzly voice says, "You're in the right place. He's there." Tom smiles, says, "Got it." and heads back to his date.

They finish their meal, walk back, and say good night. But before Tom goes up to his room, he turns around and lays a sweet kiss on Keira's trembling lips, and they continue to kiss for a few more minutes. "See you tomorrow sweet heart." He says, and then he goes to bed. Keira smiles as she watches him walk away. She looks down at her watch and nearly jumps when she sees it's 9:59. Right as Tom walks into his room, Brad emerges from the room next door. He looks down at Keira, "Right on time." He says, and then slides down the stair railing. Keira nervously agrees and feels a bit awkward, but is put at ease when Brad approaches her, lifts her off the ground, and playfully carries her over his shoulder. They laugh for a moment and he sets her down. They stare into each other's eyes. There is magic between them. But is it as magic as what she and Tom have? We don't know yet, and neither does she.

"You hungry?" Brad asks. "Oh... Well, um..." She stumbles. "Yeah me neither... You ever swim around here?" Brad asks. "Not often, and never at night." Keira says. "Well there's a first time for everything.

Isn't there?" Brad says. We watch as Brad and Keira swim and play, naked, though not making contact with each other, so not sexual, in the beautiful nighttime ocean. Brad gets out to dry off, and as he walks towards the towels, we see he's looking at a message on his hi-tec digital wristwatch, that reads, "He is there. All systems go." Brad smiles, types a message back, "Clear. Thanks." and he and Keira dry off, dress, and head back to the hotel. Brad tells Keira good night, and she holds onto his hand as he leaves. He turns looks at her for a moment, and then kisses her. She is torn, but then goes with it. They say good night, and Keira smiles as she watches Brad head into his room. What a night... Keira walks back to her place, but we stay on the hotel. We slowly begin to zoom towards Tom's room, and as we get close, we see that there is a sliver of an opening in the window curtains, and as we zoom even closer, we see Tom's eye looking through the sliver... He saw the whole thing.

The next morning, Brad awakes and makes a cup of coffee. He yawns and puts on a robe. He decides to see what the weather's like, and when he opens the door he sees the words, '*STAY AWAY FROM MY GIRL'* written on the ground in front of his door <u>in blood</u>. The sight makes him jump, and he spills coffee all over his robe. Brad goes back into his room and closes the door behind him.

Cut to Tom, waiting in the hotel lobby. Waiting... Where's Keira? Cut to Keira, taking a shower, naked, lathering oil and soaps onto her body. Back to Tom. A few moments later, Keira arrives in the lobby, hair still wet, dressed in the sweatpants and t-shirt from the day before, but no glasses today. "Oh hello!" She says, happy to see Tom. "Hi." Tom replies, a little standoffish, then adds, "I just came by to extend my stay two nights." "Oh I'm glad you'll be sticking around!" She says. "Yeah..." Tom says unenthusiastically, putting the money on the table and heading out for the day. Keira looks around, confused by the exchange.

A little bit later Brad walks in. "Hello!" Keira says. "Um... Hi." Brad responds uneasily. "I'd just like to extend my stay a couple nights." He says. "Oh okay. Maybe we can go out again tonight?" She asks. "Well... I don't... I've got something to do tonight." Brad says. It is apparent he'd like to spend the evening with her, but is worried about the message he saw in front of his door. "Oh. All right..." Keira replies. Brad pays and leaves, and Keira doesn't know what to make of the two exchanges.

Meanwhile, Tom is standing on the roof of a building, wearing a bulletproof vest, machinegun in hand. He presses a button on his glasses, and we see his POV, a red dot walking across a map. Cut to Brad, dressed in a similar bulletproof vest, holding his sniper rifle, walking across the town. Tom props his gun over the side of the building, and as he watches the red dot move, he aims his gun at the spot near the bottom of another building, where the person that is the red dot should soon be appearing. Brad stops walking for a moment (we cut to the glasses POV of the red dot stopping, and snap back to Brad) and he says into his watch, "Activate radar jammer." Then Brad heads up the stairs to the top of another building. We cut to Tom. "What? How could I lose him?" He says to himself. He presses a button on his glasses and says, "Activate radar mixer." Now we see Brad, on the other roof, looking at his watch in confusion. Both men frustratedly sigh and lay on their respective roofs in defeat.

Later that day Tom heads back to his room. He takes off his vest, stows it and his gun away, and lies on his bed. He's obviously had a long day. He dozes off, and is awoken by knocking on his door. He gets up and opens it, revealing Keira, holding a tray full of homemade food. "What do you want?" Tom asks drearily. "I just came to bring you this... I cooked it for you myself. It's Sheppard pie and green beans. My old auntie's recipe." She looks at Tom with longing eyes. "Come in." He says, and steps aside, letting her in and closing the door behind them.

Cut to twenty minutes later, they're eating and laughing and enjoying themselves. "Listen... I really like you." Tom says. "I really like you." Keira replies. Tom thinks for a moment, and decides it'd be best to clear the air about what he saw the night before, "Can I ask you something?" he starts. Keira is about to answer when her beeper starts beeping. "Oh, gotta go. Got a costumer that needs something." Tom sighs, but as he watches her go, he can't help but feel a little cheered up.

Keira walks into the lobby and finds Brad leaning on the counter. "Oh hey." He says. "Hello." She says, not sure how to handle the situation, torn between the two men, though now favoring Tom. "It looks like my plans fell through for the night. Want to get dinner?" Brad says, not letting any threatening message stand in the way of potential love. "Oh... I, uh..." She starts, struggling with what to say. Brad makes a funny face, mocking her, and this makes her laugh a little. He does a silly, yet charming little dance, and she laughs more. The tension is eased and she's softening up to him. At the same time, deep down, this just makes things harder. "So whaddya say?" He asks. "Oh, all right." She says. This brings a smile to Brad's face, and he wraps his arms around her. They embrace, and before they know it, before Keira can even think to stop herself, they begin to kiss. They begin to kiss deeply, and not five seconds go by, before a voice says, "What's this?" Brad and Keira look up. Tom is standing at the entrance to the lobby. Keira lets go of Brad, but he's still got his arms around her. "I... I'm sorry!" She says to Tom, and then looks at Brad and whispers, "I'm so sorry." "Is that the man you were with last night?" Tom asks. "But— how did you— who told—" Keira stumbles. "Stop." Tom says. "I knew it was too good to be true with you. If he's the one that makes you happy, then be with him. Be with each other." Brad looks at Keira, still holding her. "Is this man your boyfriend?" He asks. "No, we just—" She starts before Tom cuts in, "No... We just had one beautiful dinner together. That's it. The best night of— But you guys should be together. That's the way it's meant to be." Brad and Keira look at each other, then Brad looks at Tom. "Well, thanks." He says. Tom winks, "Don't mention it." The gesture is from the heart. He genuinely wants Keira to be happy, and he can tell Brad isn't a bad guy. Brad smiles at him, and Tom smiles back. Brad turns back to Keira and they kiss. He then looks up at Tom, who is about to go back to his room, and says, "We were gonna go grab some dinner tonight if you want to join us?" Tom thinks for a second. "Well... I couldn't... uh—" Tom stops, and watches Brad, who has started to make the same playfully mocking face at him that he made at Keira moments before. Brad then does the same silly, yet charming dance, and it works again, Tom can't help but start laughing. Keira sees and starts laughing too, and soon they're all laughing together.

Cut to the three of them laughing and enjoying a nice dinner together at the restaurant from the previous night. Keira eats meatloaf, Tom eats pizza, and Brad hilariously has made the mistake of ordering the shrimp that Tom had so much trouble with the night before. The laughing settles for a moment, and Brad sweetly gives Keira a gentle kiss. Even though he wishes it was him Keira was kissing, Tom smiles as he watches this, happy for Keira, and for his new friend, Brad.

The three of them walk back to the hotel. Brad holds hands with Keira, and throws his arm over Tom's shoulder in a friendly manner. As they arrive, before going their separate ways, they stand, looking at each other. Brad speaks. "To love…" he says, and then kisses Keira. "And to friendship." he says, extending his hand to Tom, who gladly accepts and shakes it. "Come on, we can walk up together." Tom says to Brad. "I'll join you in one second. I just want to tell Keira good night." Brad replies. Tom goes and waits by the stairs, leaving Brad and Keira with a moment alone. "Listen," Brad says, "I love you." Keira looks at him, smiles, and gives him a kiss. Brad wanted her to return his 'I love you' with one of her own, but this will do for now. He smiles at her and watches her as she walks to the lobby. Before opening the door, she looks over her shoulder and smiles at him, then disappears inside.

Brad meets Tom at the stairs. "What'd you guys say?" Tom asks, genuinely caring about their relationship. "It was all good stuff." Brad says and chuckles. The men arrive at their doors. "Listen man, I can't tell you how much I apprec—" Brad starts before Tom cuts him off, "Don't even mention it. After watching you two, I don't regret my decision for a second. And hey, I made a new friend in the process." Tom smiles at Brad, and gives him a wink. Brad appreciates this gesture, and returns the wink with one of his own. Tom enters his room and closes his door. As Brad opens his door and steps inside, he takes a look down at the ground, and sees that the message that was written there this morning, has faded away…

The next day Brad awakes to a beeping wristwatch. He looks at it and reads a message, "Must execute mission today, or all is lost. Will send photos later." Brad hops out of bed and gets ready to take care of business.

In the room next door, Tom's sunglasses vibrate on the dresser next to his bed. He wakes up, presses a button on them, and the same deep, grisly voice from earlier comes out, "You must finish what you went there to do, today. Have you seen the target man yet?" "Not yet, I came close yesterday, but then my radar got jammed." Tom replies as he gets out of bed and slips into his mission clothes. "Okay, well we'll be sending you some photos of the target shortly. This should help you to identify and take him down more easily." "*Exquisite.*" Tom says and smiles to himself as he zips up his black nylon body suit, puts on the glasses, and cocks his gun.

Brad is dressed in a similar body suit, although his is burnt orange and maroon. He stands in the lobby, speaking with Keira. "Listen." He says. "I've got some business to take care of today. I might not be back until late, but I will be back. Okay?" "Yeah." Keira says and laughs. "Why so serious?" She asks, not grasping the magnitude of the situation. Brad cracks a smile and kisses her. "I love you." He says and waits. She doesn't say it back, but she kisses him deeply and passionately. "What's this?" a voice off screen says. Brad and Keira look up to see Tom, just like yesterday, only today, they all burst out laughing. "Just the man I wanted to see!" Brad says. "Come here." Tom says back, and waves him over. Brad goes to him and they hug. "You're a good guy." Brad says to Tom. Tom smiles at him. "Listen you guys... There are some things I've got to do today, so I might not be able to join you two for lunch or dinner. But I want you to know I really appreciate you guys." Tom says. "Well I'm waiting for a... fax." Brad starts, "Why don't we all hang out for a little bit? I mean, if you've got time, of course." He says to Tom and Keira. "Yeah... I'd love to. I'm actually waiting for something too." Tom says and takes a seat. "Well, I've got to be at work actually." Keira starts. "Oh wait... work is right here!" They all laugh at Keira's joke (they're in the hotel lobby where she works).

We watch a quick montage of them talking, laughing, and enjoying they're time. Then, Tom and Brad both take a break from the conversation to look at the info coming into their sunglasses and wristwatch respectively.

Tom's eyes go wide as he looks into his sunglasses. We cut to his POV. A photo of Brad. Brad's eyes go wide as he looks at his wristwatch. We cut to his POV. A photo of Tom. It dawns on them... one of them is going to have to kill the other.

They reach for their guns. Tom has his out and pointed at Brad's head, first. Brad has his hand on his gun, but it isn't even out of the holster yet. Keira looks on in wide-eyed shock. Brad looks at Tom. Tom looks at Brad. They stare into each other's eyes. A tiny smile of understanding appears on Brad's face, and he gives Tom a small nod. Tom returns the tiny smile, gives Brad a wink... a tear rolls down Brad's face... and Tom pulls the trigger, blasting Brad's face and head to pieces.

Keira shrieks, Tom shudders, Brad's headless body falls to the floor. Keira begins sobbing and runs to Tom, who wraps his arms around her and softly cries one solemn tear into her shoulder. "I love you." Tom whispers in her ear. "I love you so much." He says. Keira's sobs slow down. She moves her hands from Tom's back to over his heart. She stays like this for a few moments, her crying ceases, and she says, "Your heart beats in synch with the tides of life... I've always wanted to sail the tides of life." Tom looks at her, then he smiles. Keira smiles back, and for the first time in the movie she says, "I love you."

The End.

Slam cut to credits.
At the very end of the credits there is a bumper.
The bumper is Tom and Keira in the mission headquarters. The president of the company tells Tom the destination of his next mission. Paris.

* * *

*"Write a self-help book"*
[I wrote that in my journal sometime during my trip through Mexico in December 2011.]

Note: I acted in two movies that were each released in March 2012. Project X was released on March 2nd, and went on to make 102 million dollars worldwide. 21 Jump Street was released on March 16th, and went on to make 201 million dollars worldwide.

[I came up with the title (<u>I'm Just Sitting on a Fence</u>), subtitle (*The secrets of life.*), cover idea (the old picture of me on the fence), and self-help memoir concept for this book all in one day in April 2012, about a month after I began writing stories for it. I wrote in my journal that it'd be "*a travel memoir/self-help book (and a general educational tool)*".]

Note: I posted my first YouTube videos on January 2nd 2007, when I was a freshman in high school. I currently (roughly six and a half years later) have 153 videos posted, and they've received a total of about 42,000,000 views. 147 of those videos were posted within two years of that first video, and at that point they'd already received about 32,000,000 views.

[I wrote *How to read this book.* sometime during the month of June 2012.]

* * *

# August Diaries

## 8/2 [2012]

When I woke up this morning—my first in the hostel—I was thinking in bed about how I'd like to start being more outgoing, like I was in the old days. As I lay there, I had an impulse, or a whim, and I just went with it. I just said, gently, "Rise and shine. Rise and shine sweethearts." I just let myself say it. Five or six of my hostel roommates were awake and not in the room, but I was talking to the one guy and the girl that were still sleeping in their bunks across from mine and next to mine, and I raised my vocal level a little, and said again, "Rise and shine sweethearts. Rise and shine." The guy moved a little, so I got down off of my bunk and walked to his. I was hoping that I could maybe wake them up (it was already about 10), and then we could talk and maybe even bond since we were the only three in the room, and then if that worked out I could take them to the Coit Tower and show them around San Francisco, since I was here just a couple years ago. I was unsure about it, but kind of wanted to pursue my whim. I gently started to rock the guy's bunk to provoke some squeaking noises from the frame. It squeaked and he started to move, so I stopped rocking it. He propped up onto his elbows, lifted his head, and I meant to smile at him, but his face was so, just baffled, it shook me, and I pretended I had not been talking to him, and I just turned and climbed back in my bunk and just laid there for five minutes then left the room, and that was it. I wanted to wake them up, to follow through on the whim, to see if it would work, but I was afraid. I didn't know if he or the girl would be bitter at me for waking them.
Today though, even though I tried not to be, I was discouraged by this episode, because I kept telling myself I should have just taken the chance, taken a risk. I would be walking, and I wouldn't be enjoying myself fully because I would think about how I could possibly be walk-ing with the two roommates. It made me feel kind of like I didn't exist. Also, I was at the art museum, and some guy who was my age said with a Spanish accent, "You're the guy from the movies." and I said yes and

we shook hands and I walked on. About ten minutes later he approached me and asked if he could take a photo with me. I said yes and as his mom got the camera ready on her Iphone, we were just standing next to eachother and waiting and he asked me, "What movie are you in?" I said, "Jump Street." and he said, "Yes, Jump Street...... and Scott Pilgrim?" I began to nod yes because I hadn't registered what he asked (because his English was not excellent, he was from Mexico City) and then I realized what he said, so I said, "No, oh no. I'm not— that's not— you're thinking of Michael Cera." He was confused. I was too humiliated to explain that that was a different person than me, we just took the photo and he said thanks and then I walked around the museum. But yeah, as I already said, I didn't enjoy it much. Anyways, I think I would like to start being more outgoing and less worrisome.

...

I used to be very outgoing. I'd take risks and face much rejection, but sometimes there was success. The thing is, I worry about coming across as strange. I never used to give much thought to that, at least not until afterward. So, I think I just want to start being more outgoing. Tomorrow I would like to bond with somebody, that's my goal.

8/4

I am at the whole foods on 4th street right now. I just ate my food and it was good. I am feeling kind of helpless right now. I feel like I have a hole in me. Less so than earlier today, but still. I just don't really know what I'm going to do with my life. I don't know.

...

I've just been sitting here for 30 or 40 minutes now, and I feel like the hole is starting to pass. I've just been sitting here thinking, and even though I haven't come up with any solutions to my worries, I find that the hole has started to fade from my soul quite a bit.

...

I do need to figure out what to do with my life though. Some kind of actual prospect. I am sitting at a table, and sitting two chairs down from me, the latin man with the Whole Foods hat on is holding a

partly-eaten banana, by his crotch. I can't tell if he's doing it intentionally or not. He's looking at his I-pad on the table, so his attention is not
blatantly on the banana, but he's holding it in the exact spot that his
p**is would be. I stood briefly to look at the screen and he's just on
ESPN.com, not porn. It's probably just a coincidence then that he has it
held there.

...

I was a little more outgoing yesterday. I had a brief conversation with
two girls from the hostel at dinner. I will continue to be more outgoing,
and I will continue to figure out my life.

8/5

Two people recognized me from 21 Jump Street in the morning, and in
the afternoon I took the ferry/bus to Muir Woods. There's a seven dol-
lar entrance fee, but no one guards the entrance, so I actually just
walked right in without paying, and I didn't even care. I was quite hungry, so before exploring through the park, I went and got a sandwich
from the café. It was a decently enjoyable sandwich, and after I finished it, I went out and enjoyed the beautiful park. The park looked
kind of prehistoric, like dinosaurs could have lived there. It'd be a decent place for a dinosaur movie. I also wrote a poem there. Here it is:
Moss covered trees, a perfect breeze. Redwoods so high, a nice blue
sky. Chirp of a bird, speechless for the right word. Full of life these
Muir Woods are. Shivers up my spine, tingles to linger. "Son you are
home," to me the forest whispers.
I wrote that when I reached this one point of the park where no one
was around and it was completely silent. It was so nice.

...

Oh and at the park, I remembered that I never wrote about the time I
went skydiving, and it's kind of interesting, because I pretty much
fainted when we exited. I was blacked out for about thirty seconds as
me and the instructor on my back free fell, and I could feel everything,
I just couldn't see for a bit and I was half-dazed. My vision returned
right at the end of the free fall when the instructor pulled the rip cord

75

to release the parachute and we began to float down, and I just dangled from the instructor for a bit—too overwhelmed to even be overwhelmed—until I came out of my daze and registered my situation, and how crazy it was, and then, how cool it was. I'd gone because I'd been taking a solo roadtrip through Florida at the time, and I was going through a kind of quarter life crisis during that trip (It was about maybe a year and a half ago, in Florida City). The guy who was on my back told me afterward that I had been like resisting when we were exiting the plane and he had to force us out, and I hadn't even realized I was doing it, but he said I was trying to grab hold of the sides of the exit. It was pretty interesting.

## 8/7

First of all, I am at the library. I had an altercation a few moments ago. So, I had just finished looking at the California travel books, I was on the third floor, and I was waiting for an elevator. As I'm waiting, a tall guy walks up by me to wait for it too. So the elevator comes, and since I'm closer to it, the guy is staying back a little so I can get on first. The doors open and there are about 4 or 5 people in it. I do not go in immediately because I assume that some of them must be getting out. They are not getting out though, so I begin to walk in. As I walk in, a shabby looking man standing in the middle of the elevator, possibly a hobo, looks at the man behind me and starts to make a motion with his hand, pointing towards the ground and moving his arm up and down to signal that the elevator is going down. So, I am now fully entered into the elevator and the tall man who was behind me is now walking in and he says to the old man, "I was waiting for him." Him meaning me. Shocked, I turn to him and say, "Don't throw me under the bus." (I was actually very surprised to hear these words as they left my mouth. I didn't think. I just said it.) He looked at me and responded, "I was just telling him…" "Oh, so you're just gonna switch the blame on every person?" I asked with a raised voice. "Cool down." The hobo said to me. I looked at him, then at the tall man, who had ignored my previous question, then I turned and shook my head. A second later the elevator arrived at the first floor. The tall guy was the first out and I was next. I watched him for a moment as he walked and then I followed close behind him. (He had on green jeans, he looked 25 or 27, and he had a hip black moustache and glasses. And I mean, really I could have seen us getting along quite well based on how he looked. He'd thrown salt in my eyes though. For no reason.) So, I followed right behind him and then I said, "Hey. Glad you didn't have any trouble waiting— figuring out how to exit an *el-ev-ator*." He turned, saw me, and said, "You better forget it." By the way he said it I could tell that it was supposed to be like a warning. As I said, he was tall, probably 6'5", but I was not intimidated by his height—I could have broken his arm if I'd grabbed his shoulder with one hand and his wrist with the other, then hit my knee into the back of his elbow. But, he said this, I paused, and he started to walk away. So, I said, "Well just can't you say sorry?" He completely ignored me and left, right through the lobby and out the automatic door as I stood there, just dumbfounded, about, all of the whole situation……

I don't know where that came from. It's, kind of wild. Maybe since I've been more outgoing I was quicker to stand up for myself. I've also been overwhelmed all day because my hostel is booked up this weekend.

…

I think I've recognized what the problem is that has been plaguing me the past couple of years. I've been afraid of outbursts like this, and so I've quieted myself. By doing so, I've achieved the goal of coming across as respectable and generous, but inside I think my bitterness grows, it's just not visible on the surface. The bitterness' source…?

But this is the first, or the most extreme, thing to happen like this in a couple years. Maybe it's correlated to my recent decision to be more outgoing. It must be. But should I now withdraw? No… I should go forward.

It does feel risky. It feels uncomfortable, but I cannot reach my potential if I do not explore the once familiar (but now a forgotten dream) field of outgoing interaction. My mind has grown so much since those days, I am so wise, so if I am able to recapture comfort in the outgoing, life will be so pleasant, because it will be like mixing two perfect complimentary ingredients—a wise mind and a fearless/striking personality. I think it's a possibility that I'll have to endure more episodes such as this, and that unpredictability really isn't a fun way to live, but I think I will get there, and when I do, I will <u>flourish</u>. (Blossom. Forge on! The strength is in *you*.)

...

I think instability is the frequent culprit of my bitterness. Is it coincidence that this angry episode comes on the day that I find out that I have nowhere to stay this weekend? I think not. Maybe I need to make more solid plans in the future. Or something?

...

As I was walking down 4th street, I gave 75 cents to a homeless man. He was just sitting there reading a book and I reached out and gave it to him. He was grateful. I know it's not much, basically nothing, but that is the first time I've given money to a homeless person in years (and to him that's like four dollars). I felt so good doing it too, so generous (even if it was not much), and I think it is a positive product of my outgoingness. So, while I will have to endure some uncomfort during this pursuit of outgoingness, I can also be treated to little pleasures like this... Excellent, really. Progress.


8/8

Progress: When I walk by a strip club I will typically hold my breath until I have passed it. But today, this promoter standing outside the door of this club said to me as I walked down the sidewalk in his direction, "Can I have a second of your time?" I ignored him and walked faster. As I neared closer to him, he repeated the question, and this time I shook my head firmly. I kept walking, and he asked one more time as I passed by, this time adding, "Just *one* second." and I turned and said, "You just did." (As in, "You just did have <u>one second</u> of my time.") It really was funny and quite outgoing. The joke just popped into my head and I said it without thinking. I find this to be a good and encouraging moment for myself. A sly but lighthearted zinger, improvised on the spot, delivered right in public. The delivery wasn't even that shy. A step in the right direction.

I was not going to write about today because I did not make much progress. I was quite the opposite of outgoing, because I stayed inside all day making this audition tape for this Vince Vaughn movie called Starbuck. It took about 5 hours to make the tape, plus another hour for eating/restroom/misc. Hopefully they will like it.

Well, what made me end up writing this diary, is this: I came to Whole Foods to eat and use their WiFi to e-mail the tape to my manager. After I finished my food, I was sitting and waiting for my audition to upload so I could send it, and I got recognized by none other than professional Major League baseball pitcher Tim Lincecum of the San Francisco Giants. He complimented my performance in the movie (I didn't hear which one he said he saw) and we shook hands, so I got to touch his pitching hand. And I was kind of flattered by him recognizing me. Tomorrow I travel to a hostel in Montara by way of bus, where I will stay for four nights and get some rest.

...

Regression: In City Lights bookstore, I was sitting and reading on the upstairs level, there was this girl walking around, and from where I was sitting I could not tell if she was much older than me, but she looked fashionable and somewhat cute. She browsed the poetry books for a minute, and then, while I was looking at my book, she walked over to me and politely asked, "Do you work here, or are you just reading?" "No, I'm just reading." I told her, and we smiled at each other at the same time. I realized then that she was beautiful, ravishing, I saw it in her smile, a smile I cannot describe with any cliché, a smile that spoke to me, and as she walked away I pictured myself spending the rest of my life with her. There was a mutual connection. [Line from 'This Magic Moment': "And I knew that you felt it too, by the look in your eyes."]. She turned and walked down the stairs and I tried to read, but I couldn't re-focus on my book. I was ruined. A couple minutes later, she came back up the stairs and continued browsing (I assumed she went downstairs to ask an employee a question). It was just me, her, and this one other girl who was also reading, in the upstairs room. I glanced at her occasionally as she browsed. Then, after a minute, the other girl in the room stopped reading, gathered her books and bag, and walked downstairs, leaving just me and the beautiful girl, alone. The girl walked across to my side of the room and scanned the books on the shelf nearest me. She was standing less than fifteen feet away. I could tell she wanted me to talk to her. The way she scanned the books. I knew it. I pretended to read and my breathing became heavy. I did want to talk to her, I really thought, based on that one brief interaction, that we could have been in love, honestly, but I just couldn't regulate my breathing or understand my mind. Then, a guy and a lady came up the stairs together, and since we were no longer alone, I knew the chance was over. The girl, possibly the love of my life (and I can never know), left a minute later...


8/10

I must write this. So, when I woke up this morning, I thought about the girl from yesterday. I thought about how I'd never know what could have been, but in a less despairing way than yesterday. I said to myself—she was a rare one, but there are more out there who could be my love, and who knows, maybe we will cross paths again if we are meant to be together. I had a positive attitude. So I showered, did a few stretches, and went down to get breakfast in the ballroom. I prepared some eggs and oatmeal, then I waited in line for fruit, right behind some girl with green pants. She got fruit and moved on, and then I got fruit and took a seat at a half-occupied round table where three other people were sitting. The three people were already having a conversation, so I didn't talk to them. I looked out across the room at the breakfasting hostellers, and, who do I see...? I see the girl from City Lights. She walked and took a seat at a table with two friends. She had been the one who was right in front of me in the fruit line, with green pants, and I hadn't even realized. This may seem unlikely, but here's the thing, City Lights bookstore is only like a block away from this hostel. It was like the movie Serendipity. I knew I had to talk to her, I definitely had to, but I felt too awkward to go up and sit with her and her friends, so I decided I'd wait until she finished her food and went to the kitchen to clean her dishes and then I'd approach her. I waited. After about ten minutes, she and her friends got up to clean their dishes, and I followed. As they washed them, I dumped my food into the trash (actually, I'd only been able to finish about half of it since I'd vastly decreased my eating rate when I'd noticed the girl, but it was worth it to waste it to get a chance to talk to her). The girl put away her plate, grabbed a cup, and approached the tea station next to the trashcan. She was right next to me. I scraped the last of the oatmeal into the trash then turned to her and said, "Were you at—" She backed away, thinking I was trying to get some tea from the station. I was rattled for half-a-second, but then I tried again, "Were you at City Lights bookstore last night?" She looked at me, smiled, and said, "Yeah... How are you?" I wasn't sure if she recognized me or not. "Good." I told her, then I observed, "It's a good bookstore." "Yeah it is." She said, smiling. "Do you like your breakfast?" I said. "Yeah, it's good. It's free." After she said that, the conversation was naturally over.  She seemed very nice, but I didn't know what else to say. I didn't see the same connection in her eye as I had last night, and we said bye. But, I wasn't upset by this. She seemed very sweet, and I'm super glad I got to talk to her. I can do anything. Now I will leave and catch the BART/bus out of town to Montara.


8/15

I am back in SF. Montara was good. The hostel was in a good location, right by the ocean. I felt a mixture of emotions during my time there, and went back and forth between progress and regress.
My first day there was uneventful, I just arrived around seven or eight, ate dinner, said hello to the two families that were also staying there, and went to sleep. On my second day, I went for a hike, and then went to a sandwich place and had a nice sandwich. I was feeling kind of stressed and secluded the whole time though. When I got back to the hostel, I went and looked at the ocean. As I stared at it—the waves crashing against the rocks and jutting cliffs, the birds swiftly gliding a

few feet above the surface—I had an epiphany, something along the lines of: birds don't know everything, the ocean doesn't know everything, and humans don't know everything either, and I was suddenly filled with great energy. I hacked up a loogie and spit it into the sea (like Jack Dawson), then went running across the rocks. I came to a halt and let out a quick yell of freedom to the sky. Then I screamed a little to the birds and across the ocean and my stresses disappeared. I felt like my shell had finally shattered and I was free. It was great. But just as quickly as the energy came, it dissolved, and a few minutes later I was lying face down in the sand, balling my eyes out uncontrollably for no reason. That evening, I was sitting alone at the kitchen table, looking at my computer, and this old lady, about one-hundred, slowly walked in with a walker and sat down next to me. She was wearing a cloth night gown that fit her body loosely, her skin was infinitely wrinkled and blotched red, her hair was very thin and white, her eyes were brown with a bluish-grey outline around the iris' and by the pupils, and she shook continuously. She was sort of scary to witness, because you couldn't tell if she was dying or not. I was nervous to be sitting next to her. She sat there, not doing anything in particular, just wheezing as she inhaled, moaning as she exhaled, and shaking the whole time. When she started to cough a little, I wanted to ask if she was okay, but I didn't want to offend her. After the coughing passed, I waited a moment, then asked, "Where are you from?" She turned her head a little, but couldn't turn it all the way in my direction, so she mostly turned her eyes, and said, "What?" She had an old-lady-ish, but high-pitched voice. "Where are you from?" I repeated. She looked down and just continued to wheeze and moan for a moment, and then she turned her eyes back to me and again said, "What?" I began to feel self-conscious and wanted to abort the conversation, but I didn't want to hurt her feelings, and I raised my voice asked again, "Where are you from?" This time she replied, "Sacramento." I could tell that based on the casualness of her answer that she was okay, that the shaking and everything was just part of her daily condition, so I no longer was worried that she was dying or something and just said, "Okay, cool." "What?" She asked. "Oh, nice to meet you." I told her. She smiled a little, breathed, and asked, "Are you from here?" "No, I'm just travelling."

She didn't hear what I said so I repeated it louder. "That's good." She said. I began to ask her how long she would be here, but she then said, "Well enjoy it," and she half-smiled and struggled up from her chair to her walker, "Life flies…" …Life flies… This comment was simple, but it meant something to me. It seemed like such a wise, angel thing to say. When she said that, she seemed, almost, angelic. I was really grateful at that moment that the conversation had happened. I said thanks and have a good night, and she turned and slowly made her way out of the kitchen and down the hall. After that talk I felt a little clearer in the mind.

I would say days three and four were semi-fine days for the most part, except, as a side note, there was this heavyset woman of fifty-seven years that was talking to me for about one or two hours in the hostel lounge about the politics of social security and her daughter's college experience, and the whole time all I said was, "Yeah." or, "Oh." or I just nodded because I couldn't find a way to end it, and she seemed like a pervert.

Anyways, I think what I got from my weekend was that I think I'm just going to stop *worrying* myself about being outgoing, and I'm just going to start focusing on being positive and happy.


8/16

Progress: I am walking down Mission Street, taking some photos, I am feeling happy, and I think that is positive. ; )


8/17

San Francisco. I love San Francisco. This morning I woke up from some good dream, I laid in the bunk bed, and I began to think about how I was born as a little baby and then I grew into this, into me. It made me think about how life is beautiful. As I was lying there, my roommate, a tall and plump Asian technology student from Australia, came into the room holding a bagel with cream cheese on it in a napkin. I looked over the side of my bunk at him as he took a seat on the floor against the wall, pulled out his I-pad, and bit into the bagel, and I said to him, "Sorry, actually there's no eating in the rooms." I wasn't trying to have a power trip or anything, I just wanted to let him know since it appeared he didn't. "Oh it's all right, mate. Just a bagel." He replied, glancing up at me. "Yeah, well the bagel might produce a lot of crumbs... Doesn't it?" He stared at me for a moment with a somewhat perplexed look on his face, then he turned back to his I-pad and took another bite of his bagel. His eyes flicked nervously in my direction a few times as I watched him eat a couple more bites, then, noticing the mini-trashcan on his right, I suggested, "Why don't you take your bites over the trashcan right beside you?" "I think it's fine, mate." He said, almost aggressively. "Well... I'm just telling you because they told me not to eat in here yesterday. I agree with you, but I don't want you to get in trouble... You can put the trash can in your lap, even." "Alright," he said, turning away from me, "I'll eat over the bin..." "Cool. Sorry about that." You know, these past few days, I've been focusing on the positives, and little negative things have occasionally happened, but I've been happy, and I haven't been *worrying* about being outgoing. At the same time, something like that interaction, I feel, is a carryover from my pursuit of outgoingness. I've found myself being a bit more bold a couple times; like, telling him about the no eating in the room, I probably wouldn't have done that a few weeks ago. So I've found a good balance. It's positive. And I was glad that he listened to me (And he did; every time I'd briefly watch him as he took a bite, he took it over the trashcan, or over the "bin", as they call it.) because literally just yesterday a cleaning lady came into the room while I was looking out the window, eating cashews, and she told me I couldn't eat in the room because of crumbs and such. So it wouldn't have been fair if he'd been able to eat his bagel. Today is Friday, and tomorrow I'm going to Yosemite National Park for five nights. But yes, I see the progress, and I am very grateful for it.

...

My plan for today is to walk around and observe the architecture/atmosphere/scenery of the city, and to look for a sweet woman to chat with.

...

What I observed:

I observed a family of French tourists in Japan-town cracking up as they watched a classily dressed thirty year old black man dancing his heart out for an invisible audience. I don't think he was crazy, he didn't seem like it, he maybe just desperately wanted to be a pop star.

I observed a pigeon on my bench admiring me momentarily with its sweet little eye.

I observed a Spanish girl softly crying as she casually browsed the books in City Lights bookstore.

I observed these two guys around my age who recognized me on a street corner outside of City Lights bookstore. They told me they'd seen 21 Jump Street and it was nice meeting me, and, in an slightly uncomfortable attempt to be a role model, I told them to think positively and believe in themselves and they could do whatever, and they seemed unconvinced or something but said thanks. It's awkward to try and be a role model to someone your own age. They saw me more as a peer. It's not like they even asked for the advice, I just feel the pressure to advise when I'm recognized. But no biggie.

...

I was in my hostel bed, I'd just sent an e-mail to my parents informing them of my Yosemite plans, and a possibly worrisome thought occurred to me. I realized that what I did today—walking around, observing, looking for a girl—is what I do most every day, and I think that is... pointless? I don't know. I don't really do anything. But what should I do? I am not worried about this, but I am not sure about it.


8/20

Yosemite's a beautiful place. Yesterday I did a 9.2-mile hike (round-trip) up to Glacier Point, which gave me confidence in my physical abilities. It was so strenuous, but I aced it. Today I went again to Yosemite, and on the bus ride there (I'm staying roughly 25 miles away) two people from my hostel invited me to join them on their hike. I accepted. The girl of the pair was a twenty-five year old German, the guy was a twenty-eight year old from Portugal, they both spoke English fluently (the girl a tad bit better than the guy), and they met in San Diego a few days ago. At the park we hiked around Mirror Lake and the Lower Yosemite Trail, and we returned to the hostel around seven. It was a nice day. The squirrels are pretty comfortable with humans, and I almost hit one with a rock. I was not expecting or trying to hit it. Then I almost hit the guy from Portugal with a rock in his back accidentally when he was wading shirtless in the river and I was skipping rocks in his direction. He was just a little surprised, but I apologized profusely. Yosemite's history is not as pretty as its nature, though. Yosemite has been inhabited by humans for 800 years. Awanachee Indians were the original inhabitants. In the 1820's when the gold rush occurred, California sanctioned a sweep of the [Yosemite] valley, and the Indians were massacred and driven from their land. The wranglers believed there was gold in Yosemite, and somehow felt that this belief justified the torture and brutality they delivered upon the Indians. Within two years of the original massacres, it was confirmed that there was no gold in Yosemite, but a group of investors recognized the land's tourism potential and began to develop. The 1850's were Yosemite's heyday, the period when it was known as 'America's Playground'. They had a golf course, hotels, and ski slopes. But, any Indian that attempted to reclaim his land during this period was first tortured and then slayed. Still, into the 1900's, Yosemite thrived as a tourist destination. In the 40's, movie theatres were opened and they began to develop housing. The Indians were long gone at this point, but their legacy remains. In the 90's things finally took a turn in a positive direction when the government began to shut down the hotels, housing, golf courses, theaters, etc., and made it a point to start preserving the nature. They have continued in this positive direction since then, but the history and violent legacy that the valley holds can never be erased. I learned most of this at a nice—or, I should say, educational—exhibit they have in the visitor's center, yesterday. God, it is sad. That's the problem with America, its foundation, its roots, are based on slaughter and ramshack. Corruption. It's such a young country, yet so corrupt from the beginning. That is why the youth—i.e. me—are forever searching for a non-existent home. If I accept my roots, I am accepting the massacring of an Indian who had just been forced to watch his crops and horse burn. Indians were peaceful, very in touch with nature in a religious way, so the pain that they felt as they watched their land and animals burned is incomprehensible to us. That is sad, and that's why things need to change. It's not impossible. It's not. Someone, a leader, needs to be good, and *honest*...


## 8/21

Positive thinking, being happy, outgoingness are good, but today I can't help it, deep down I am worrying about what I'm gonna do with my life. I think I need to find someone to talk to about my worries. I really do.

Regress: A few minutes after I wrote that, the cleaning lady walked into my hostel room to start cleaning. I attempted to see if I could talk with her, but she only speaks Spanish.

I am at the hostel and not Yosemite today because I woke up with a bloody nose. It was pouring out, because of the altitude I think. Actually, I had planned to stay at the hostel anyways to give my legs a rest. My right knee joint has been aching, and I think that the cartilage is beginning to diminish. But I will go hiking again tomorrow.

...

I'm feeling better since this morning. I was down, way down, when I wrote that. I was thinking about how I need to share some of my worries so that they stop eating my insides like parasites. I was thinking how I could go try having a therapist, but that got me more down, I cried even. But then I just went about my day, and now, sitting at dinner, I have reached neutral, actually positive, because I realized I just need a girlfriend. I'm gonna get one. I really am. And, this just occurred to me, I'll need to be outgoing to get one. Beautiful. We will dance through life, we will talk to each other, and I can provide her with boundless love. I also am going to make a few good friends in that process.

8/22

I have been cursing all the time in my head lately. I just do. I don't want
to. I hiked up to Nevada falls, unsure the whole time. It was beautiful
but I didn't enjoy it. I've been having troublesome thoughts. I just need
to relax, that's all.

...

Relax.......................

8/23

My mom e-mailed me last night and told me an interesting development. I could not talk on the phone. My biological grandpa I've never
met (she has, I've known of him for six years) who lives by San Francisco, wants to meet me next week (my half-uncle and half-cousins
too). I think I am going to do it. Go meet him. That's interesting.

...

I think I am going through a nervous breakdown. And I don't know
what to do about it. I cried right in the public street today, I couldn't
help it. It was briefly, but I never do that...

I don't know. I don't know how I am going to end the diaries...

ha........................t a........di............ly is

end...

# Bonnie

*The secrets of life.*

I'm an SSI certified scuba diver. I got my certification on the Thai island of Koh Tao just over a year ago. A couple weeks after I got back to the U.S. from that trip, I wrote a few stories and then decided to start writing this book. The second story I wrote was a scuba diving one called *Horror and Triumph in the Mexican Ocean*. It was not about my dives in Thailand, it was about my dives in Mexico, where I first tried scuba diving during a day course on the island of Isla Mujeres about two months before the certification on Koh Tao. You will not find that story in this book, because while I was initially very proud of it, I have learned a lot about writing over this past year and no longer find it to be a top-tier story.

Writing is not the only thing that I have learned about through the process of writing this book; I have also realized things about myself that never would have occurred to me otherwise.

Yesterday I didn't know what to write, so I figured I'd have a go at rewriting *Horror and Triumph* to see if I could maybe turn into a top-tier—or at least mid-tier—story. I opened the file on Word, and as I was re-reading the intro, a short little story I'd written a few days before about my long-deceased pet goldfish hit my mind and I had a revelation of sorts.

That introduction to *Horror and Triumph in the Mexican Ocean* I'd been reading is this:

---

*I like to screw sh\*t up when I go in the ocean—when I scuba dive. I love it. I like to kick at the reefs and punch at the fish.*

*But I wasn't always so brave. When I first attempted scuba diving, it was the just about the worst experience I ever had.*

*So how did I go from hating this horrible experience to triumphing over it and thinking of it as incredible?*

*With a simple change of outlook, and a little bravery...*

---

What was it that I meant when I wrote that "I like to kick at the reefs and punch at the fish"? I meant exactly what it sounds like I meant. The day-course I took on Isla Mujeres consisted of a couple of hours spent learning about diving in a classroom, another hour or so practicing skills in a pool, and then two real scuba dives out in the ocean. Riddled with anxiety, I failed the first dive quite traumatically. (This was the *Horror.*) But after receiving some encouraging words from my German instructor Felix's female British assistant on the boat ride to the next site, I accomplished my second dive with unparalleled success. (This was the *Triumph.*) During the twenty minutes I spent swimming around under the water with Felix and my three fellow students on that second dive, a serene adrenaline unlike any I'd ever felt pumped throughout me; but Felix had to escort me from the water prematurely on account of my destructive behavior towards the ocean life (the punching). I could have felt duped about this premature exit, but I wasn't concerned about it in the least, because I was so dang proud of what I'd done.

When I wrote about all this in *Horror and Triumph*, I did so with the same pride that I'd felt while experiencing it. But as I re-read it for the first time shortly after my completion of the first draft, it momentarily occurred to me that my behavior towards the fish was maybe a little bit curious. *Why*, I wondered, *did it give me pleasure to swat at the fish?* It was slightly off-putting to ponder, so I didn't give it much thought and just went with the first theory that came to mind, which was that the adrenaline made me do it.

The revelation I had yesterday while re-reading the intro was a new theory for why I derived this 'pleasure' from disturbing the ocean life.

Before I share the theory, I need to share this little short story—the one written a few days ago involving my goldfish—about the experience that I believe explains my curious ocean behavior:

---

*Once, when I was eight, I won a pet goldfish from a pet store by success-*
*fully dropping a quarter into this small cup they had set at the bottom of*
*an empty fish tank. I loved the fish and named it Bonnie, after the girl*

*from down the street that I had a crush on. The fish was a good pet for a week, but it died after I tried to take a bath with it, because uncondi-tioned bathwater has chemicals in it that cause goldfish harm, and also because I started freaking out when I dropped it into my water and in-stinctively swatted the heavens out of it.*

---

That goldfish was the last pet I've had.

I'm an animal lover—someone who plays tug of war with dogs, teaches birds words, and teases cats with strings.

And I'm someone who can spend an hour just staring into an aquar-ium.

As I've demonstrated though, my behavior when I get the chance to interact with fish in their actual environment is nothing short of pecu-liar. I've had chances to acquire new pets since Bonnie, but I've always declined, saying I just prefer to just pet other people's dogs...

I'm scared.

That's what the revelation was—the theory.

I'm scared.

Scared to get too close to another animal.

Scared that I'll kill it.

Because it's true—I killed Bonnie. That last sentence should be laugh-able to an adult such as myself, and I could laugh it off, but something inside me really believes it to be the truth. I mean as I said, I can play with a friend's dog all day, but put me in the fish's water, where they can get as close to me as they want, and I go mad. It'd explain my fasci-nation with fish tanks (Now, I don't want to make it out to be some kind of *extreme* fascination, it's not, but I am confident that it is more intense than the average person's.), and more specifically with those transparent little fish whose skin you can look through to see their little lungs and those bones and the organs and all that *life.*

The theory is ripe with disturbing implications. There is one important detail though, that keeps me from concluding the worst and instead brings me a hopeful comfort. While I did swat at every fish that came my way, I never once made any actual contact. When I'd see one skimming along the ocean floor towards me, I'd swing my arm and send a force of water its direction that'd send it swimming right the other way. It was never my intent to harm. The swatting was just an automatic subconscious reaction to keep the fish from getting too close, where my subconscious was afraid I might do them harm, just as I had to Bonnie all those years ago.

You might be thinking it's strange that I've given all this so much thought. I know that the actual impact of this realization—the realization that for thirteen years I've been afraid of forming too deep a bond with any animal—is that moving forward in my life I might be able to a acquire and enjoy the love of a pet, and that that's not *such* a huge impact on my life, even if it is a nice one. But what got me wanting to analyze the revelation and write about it this in depth, is this other thought that came from having it—the thought that every action has a reason.

(I swatted at the fishes because deep down I was scared of hurting them.)

Why does a person say hello to a passing stranger on the street? Why do people brush their teeth? Why does a baby play in the sand? These kinds of thoughts have always been fascinating to me. I believe that people eat, drink, sleep, shower, brush their teeth, etc. because they want to be healthy and survive. But a question like 'Why does a person say hello to a stranger?' has to be thought about more in depth.

When I'm walking down the street, and I say hello to someone I don't know, I do it for a variety of reasons, but mostly I do it because I want to be friendly and improve that person's day and also to see if they're friendly as well. If it is a pretty girl, maybe I just want a chance to make eye contact, even if only for the second that it takes to say hello. But I don't always try to greet passing strangers, and why is that? Well, I suppose I don't say hello to strangers that I don't think I'd get along well with. And how do I decide who I'll get along well with? How do people decide who they like and—better yet—who they dislike?

I believe that it is in the mind that the answers to all of these questions lay. I have read a lot about neuroscience in books, and one thing that people tend to believe is that the mind has a rewards system. It rewards you for doing things that will benefit your survival and well being. It also punishes you for doing things it feels will cause you harm. This is where pleasure and pain come from.

Do you want to know why a little baby likes playing in the sand? It's because the mind feels that knowledge will increase a person's chance of survival in this world, so it gives pleasure to the little baby for discovering her environment, since she's never seen sand before. An adult is unimpressed by sand because he already knows everything he needs to know about it (It's just a harmless and inedible grain).

The reason we feel pain when we touch fire is quite obvious: because the mind is telling you you'll die if you keep your hand in that fire. But why does it hurt just as much as sticking your hand in fire when someone insults you or thinks negatively of you? Because the brain feels that social bonds are beneficial, and so it tries to teach you to improve your social skills by punishing you for missteps and rewarding you for successes.

A lot of this could be explained more in depth—with words such as cortexes and synapses—but I am not familiar enough with the technical terms to go very deep into that, as I am educated more on an amateur level. The mind is an interesting trumpet, and I feel that it can be understood when given enough time and research.

The emotional world though, is a thing unto itself. No matter how much I think about it—and even strive to master it—I can never solidly pin it down, or even really place a finger on it.

For me, trying to control my emotions would be like trying to control the weather. Yeah I can control my actions, but I can't understand the way I feel.

These past few nights I've been having a little trouble sleeping, and when I lay there in my bed before the sleep comes, my thoughts go dark. They're not about anything in particular, they're just dark.

But other times my mind is filled with a breezy lightness. These times also hit me when they want. As I mentioned, my mind's been a little bit tired these past few days, so that leads me to believe that maybe one of these light patches is on its way. Most likely I'll just be walking to the grocery store this weekend and it'll hit me.

If you're interested in knowing how one of these light patches feels, then you're in luck, because one time, as I walked from the movie theater back to my Portland hostel, I was hit with one of them and I wrote a poem as soon as I got back to commemorate it. I think it's a beautiful poem, and it's called *My most beautiful few sentences*:

---

*Sometimes you're just so happy you want to dissolve into a mist and blow away with the breeze. Your feet walk rhythmically down the sidewalk as the sun sets golden and a freight train blows its horn in the distance over the faint sound of a siren and the trees wave with the wind nice and green. Sometimes you're so calm you just disappear and everything happens.*

---

I am not sure how to conclude this story, so I think it will be fine if I just use the conclusion from *Horror and Triumph*:

---

*We dived in, made our way down the rope and swam around, looking at the corals and anemones and amazing groups of fish. I saw a pack of about 300 silver fish swimming together. I felt rock and roll music pulsing through my body the whole time. I was even laughing, I was so happy! I went down towards the bottom and started to kick the corals with my flippers. I was laughing so hard as Felix swam over to me, that it was hard to keep consistent breathing. I looked at him, floating in front of me, eyes wide, arm extended with his pointer finger waving back and forth signaling "No." and it made me laugh even more. I saw a fish swimming along the sand towards us and I punched it. I didn't get it, but it felt the force of the water and quickly swam away. It was awesome. I swam on with Felix towards the others, and as we looked at the beautiful sea plants and stuff, I continued to punch at nearby fish throughout the dive.*
*Felix took me back up a little bit before the rest of the group, and he was pretty angry that I was trying to screw life up, but I didn't care at all. I believe that if you conquer a task like that, you have the right to and*

*should celebrate. And I did. I sang sailor songs over the sound of the engine the whole ride back to shore...*

---

Actually I thought of a better way to conclude it.

I think the most important thing writing this book helped me to realize, is that no matter what is going on in my mind or emotions, as long as I have love for my family or the people around me, my heart and soul feel a little more right.

[Note: At the time that I wrote this diary, I believed it would be the last chapter (essay, story, diary...) of the book. That didn't end up being the case—there are more chapters (essays, stories, diaries...) after it. And the *P.S.* at the end is incorrect.]

Diary Entry 2/9/13 (The End)

I will write this last chapter in one sitting, as a diary entry. That's the first sentence to this diary entry. The first sentence I was previously considering using for the non-diary version of this chapter was: "In this first sentence of this last chapter, I feel compelled to write about her heart beat as she laid in my lap on the bus ride home from their dance, and how it moved me." I'd been searching for a way to end the book for a couple months when I wrote that one. It's been a couple more months since then, and I haven't really been looking for the ending lately, but now I'm just sitting down to write it. The heart beat I was referring to in that sentence belonged to an eleven or twelve year old girl that was one of the sixty children living at the orphanage I spent three weeks volunteering at this December during a five week trip through India. It was quite a trip, and my experience at the orphanage was quite an experience. I'll write about it more in a minute, but first I want to tell you where I am now.

Right now I am in the library-room of the hostel on 2nd street in Santa Monica. I'm out in LA in search of an acting job. I've been here for almost two weeks, and I've been enjoying myself quite well. About a week ago I saw a penny on the ground and picked it up for good luck, and I've picked up every penny I've come across since. It has worked. They given me good, lucky days. I don't know if I believe that it's the actual penny that provides the luck, or if it's just be a placebo that makes me think more positively, but either way it works. I have also been more relaxed around girls. When one is around me, I just think about the fact that it's my lucky day and I feel less nervous. (I put the penny in my back right pocket and carry it with me there throughout the day. You can try putting it there too if you'd like to try. There's one in the back of my brown corduroys now as I sit on it here and type all this.)

Back to India. Let me tell you, the orphanage was quite amazing. The kids, they were absolutely the best. They'd greet you with a hug, and even though there were so many of them, I ended up remembering almost all their names (except for some of the older kids I saw less often). They were funny and fun to play with too. Since returning to the U.S. I've told quite a few people that I volunteered at an orphanage in India, and a some people have responded like, "Oh, wow, that must've been intense." Really it wasn't the least bit difficult. I was staying at a hotel right near the orphanage for $5 a night, and in the morning I'd go have breakfast with the other volunteers and ask what they needed help with that day, and when they had something for me, I'd do it. I played soccer and dodgeball with the kids, we did art classes, I helped to clean the rice that we all ate a few times, and I also worked in the café they had there. I tried help with the tutoring, but I sucked at that, because they didn't really listen to me, because my presence does not exude control. So I spent three weeks there, and it was hard to say goodbye to the kids because they started to feel like family. They were so sweet and a few of them wrote me goodbye cards. Why do I write about all this in this ending diary entry here? Because my time there really affected me. Like when I mention that little girl's heart beat on the bus ride, that night I'd gone with some of them about an hour away from the orphanage to this resort where they would perform a dance once a week. And as she slept on my lap on the drive back and I could feel her heart beating, I felt like she was my little sister. They were awesome and I miss them. (Also, I want to go back and visit them again soon.)

Okay, and do you want to know the first sentence of another introduction to this last chapter that I was considering? Okay, it was this: My heart is the Taj Mahal. I came up with that sentence the day I visited the Taj Mahal. It was just so beautiful. I spent two hours inside of it. If you're not familiar with the specifics, it's a perfectly symmetrical tomb built by a maharaj for his wife who died during childbirth. You can go inside and look at their two coffins. Most people spend about 15 minutes in there, just admiring the marble walls and screens, and the gemstones engraved in the marble. I spent two hours in there, longer than anyone else I saw, because I thought, "I'm at the most beautiful building in the entire world. I can go back out to the streets of Agra (the busy city where the Taj is located), or I can spend some more time at this beautiful building, where I might never be again." It was so romantic. I'm not afraid to admit it. I even thought, "Wow... this is the embodiment of love." (That's why I wrote that sentence: My heart is the Taj Mahal.) And here's a little story to show you how inspired I was by it:

The tour guides at the Taj Mahal like to carry little mini flashlight-pens with which they light up the marble-engraved gemstones (to impress the people on the tour). I had bought this energizer mini-light (about the size of a matchbox) back in the U.S. to use during my trip for $5. I was standing in the Taj, just soaking the beauty in, when some sixty year old Indian man wearing glasses, a nice jacket, and a beanie, walked over to me, offered to give me a tour, and showed me his flashlight pen. I said no thanks and showed him that I had my own flashlight. He asked if he could see it, so I handed it to him. He played with it for a moment, and I could see he was very impressed by it. My light was much brighter than his. He asked where I'd got it. I told him I got it back home. He asked for how much. I told him 5 dollars. He offered to give me a tour for free if I'd give it to him. I said that I just wanted to stand and soak everything in. He said okay, gave it back and continued to stand beside me. We stood there a moment, then he turned to me again and offered me 100 rupees for my light. That's two dollars. He was nice about it, but I said no thanks because maybe I'd need it if there was an emergency. He looked away but continued to stand beside me. Then he turned back to me again and offered me 150 rupees. I said I couldn't do it because I might need the light for dark alleys and/or blackouts. I'd also be losing two dollars, since 150 rupees is only three dollars and I'd bought it for five. He accepted my rejection but stayed standing beside me, probably because where else was he gonna stand. I was thinking as we stood there together, and I realized that I actually did want to give him the light. Why hadn't I given it to him when he asked then? I didn't know. I knew that it was nice to have the light around in case of emergencies, but I also thought that that guy would probably use the light every day for his tours and stuff. He seemed to want it so bad. I asked him his name, and he told me it was Ali. I reached into my pocket, took out my light, and I said, "Here you go." He looked at me, accepted it, then, after thinking for a second, he reached for his money. I said, "No it's okay. You can just have it." He looked at me, and then he smiled quite genuinely. I smiled back, and a few seconds later he left. I felt so good. Really good. I did that because the Taj Mahal had filled me with love.

So the India trip was good.

Before I go, is there anything else I want to say? Really I'm pretty ready to get this book in your hands. Since you're reading this right now, it is in your hands, but it wasn't whenever I was writing this sentence. (That sentence shows that I have a good ability to think into the future—good foresight.) I've still got some re-writes I want to do, and I need to put all the dang stories in some sort of order, but you've already read them and seen the results of these future labors I'm referring to, so I don't know why I'm talking about them. Well, I like this ending. At the moment I've got four pennies in my back right pocket, and I think that's contributing to my fine writing right now. (I know I said I'd write this in one sitting, but I had to go to the store for some food, and I got three pennies in the change I received and added them to my pocket. So I wrote this in two sittings.)

I also wanted to mention my parents, because I think family is really important.

Mom—In my teens (as well as some of my youth before my teens), I thought of my mom as my enemy, and was constantly frustrated with her. Sometimes she still may frustrate me, but that is okay, because now I see that she is just a person, and I really love her; she's a very good person.

Dad—One of my Dad's best qualities is his honesty. I lie a lot, but I think subconsciously I am a very honest person, and I think I owe that to him. I love him too. Thank you dad.

Reader, it looks like this is where we part ways. I'll sure miss you, and I know you'll miss me too. [I thought of that sentence a month or so ago. That's also when I thought of this next idea.] I would like you to rip off a small piece of paper from the bottom of this page here, and I want you to keep it as a gift to remember me by. You can do whatever you want with it—even write on it—I don't care. Alright. Goodbye. I love you.

Dax


P.S. I'm going to leave you with this pretty cool story I wrote just a few days ago called The Leopards Hunted Coyotes. You'll find it on the next page.

# Women

*A lesson on respect and a lesson for women.*

"She's hot," I said as I looked at the foxy redhead with the beautiful teeth in the framed photo that sat on the desk in front of me.

The counselor looked at me with judgment in her eyes, and I wondered if it was what I'd said that she disagreed with, or that I'd said it at all.

"She's my daughter," she replied.

I blushed. I had not anticipated it. Mrs. Jones had blonde hair—not red—so how could I have known? I was skating on thin ice as it was, so I decided then that I'd keep my mouth shut nice and tight until I was spoken to, that way I couldn't dig the hole any deeper.

But what chance did I have in Mrs. Jones' office anyways? I'd been in and out of there for a pretty wide array of things ever since I arrived at the school freshman year, so I'd always be the guilty delinquent in her eyes. On this particular junior-year day though—truly—my actions that'd landed me in there had been done with the most innocent of intent. My intention had only been to make a friend, and possibly to get action. I was certainly not a crook. I could understand completely why I might have looked like a crook at that moment, back in English class, with Abby's purse in my lap and her phone stuffed down into my pocket—but it was different than it looked, all I'd wanted was Abby's number. Here, just let me explain real quickly.

We'd been working in our groups on our projects and Abby got called down to go pick something up from the front office. Abby was the girl who sat in front of me in English for a large portion of junior year (before the desks were re-arranged and I got moved behind a kid named Kevin). She was a cute girl, and I loved her (I loved a lot of girls though, so it wasn't anything too too special). So she left the room to go get whatever from the front office. I was at my desk—the only student not working with his group, because Jeff, the partner I'd been tracing for our project, had yelled at me for accidentally stepping on his genitals when he was lying on the ground (and also because I'd jokingly drawn on his face right before that with the marker I'd been tracing his outline with). Abby was out of the room, and there was her purse, sitting unattended below the desk in front of me. I looked around. Every one of my peers was pretty focused on their project. I saw an opportunity. Not an opportunity to steal any material object, not at all, but an opportunity to simply acquire Abby's phone number without the awkwardness of having to ask for it and the possibility of rejection. I slid to my knees beneath my desk, pulled the white leather bag over from under her chair, dug through it a little, found her phone, and started clicking around in search of her number. I found the screen with the number, and as I entered it into my phone, Abby walked back into the room. We made eye contact. I panicked, stuffed her phone in my pocket, kicked her purse back under her desk, and jumped up into my chair. "What are you doing with my purse?" she asked as she walked over and picked it up to inspect. Telling the truth would have embarrassed the heck out of me, because if she knew I was getting her number, she wouldn't understand, and might think I was a creep. So I said, "Nothing. I just fell down." As she inspected, she noticed the phone was gone and asked me where it was. I said I didn't know. She got the teacher involved, I was interrogated, and then I gave the phone over and was sent to the office.

"Do you respect women?" Mrs. Jones asked me.

The question caught me by surprise.

"Yes," I answered.

Mrs. Jones nodded.

I couldn't tell if she was going to say something else, so I waited.

"Well, I guess I'm just trying to figure out why you're always getting into some kind of trouble involving females."

She looked at me in a way that was both accusing and expectant. But I didn't know how to respond. I didn't know at all. I couldn't help but wonder if this was because of what I'd said about her daughter.

Mrs. Jones seemed to be considering her next question.

"Do you and your mother get along?"

"Yes," I said. "Sometimes."

She looked down at the papers on her desk, which I was worried were probably my permanent files.

"I promise I respect women," I told her.

She looked up from the papers, gave a tight-lipped smile, said, "Okay," then looked back down.

I knew she didn't believe me.

But if I look at it now, I don't know that I can blame her. Twice freshman year I'd found myself sitting there in that very office for having gotten myself into different fights with girls. (The first of these fights was a verbal fight that escalated so extremely that I actually threatened to slug the girl in the mouth after she had made a series of profanity-laced remarks about my clothing, and then the other fight was a straight fistfight between me and this girl who had about two years and one-hundred-fifty pounds on me, in which I was beaten to within an inch of my life simply because I'd run into her in the hallway and not apologized correctly.) I was always talking back to my teachers, which would help support the counselor's case, because teachers usually happen to be women. And now I was sitting there because of yet another incident involving a girl.

"I really wasn't stealing Abby's phone," I said.

"What were you trying to do?"

But what could I say? If I told her the truth about trying to get the girl's number without her knowing, she'd think I was a pervert.

"I just thought it was mine."

"Do I look stupid?"

I wasn't gonna win this one.

"I'm serious," I said timidly.

She was losing patience.

"Here's what I'm going to do. I'm going to call your mother, and she and I are going to have a conference to try and figure out why you have so much trouble behaving yourself."

I looked at my fingers in my lap. I felt small, and defenseless. I did want to tell the truth, but I couldn't, not to this witch sitting across from me.

So she and my mom had the conference. My mom came home from it quite disappointed in me. The counselor seemed to have convinced her I was a chauvinist, because that night, she and my dad sat me down and had a talk with me about the importance of respecting women. They didn't really seem to know how to tell me whatever it was they were trying to make me realize though. They had good intentions, but it was during this talk that I remember becoming convinced that I really didn't respect women, that I had some kind of unfortunate fault that made me a natural menace to females. I thought that this was what they were telling me, and I believed it. And from that point on, with this false knowledge in my head, I became very nervous and guilty around girls. I've never even been laid before, and it's probably because of this.

But I know now that what I heard them saying was untrue—that there was a miscommunication. I always did respect women just as much as I respected anyone else. The thing is though—on the whole—I didn't know how to show my respect to *anyone* all that well back then, even if I respected them to the moon and back. Like my grandmother, who died over Christmas break that junior year. She was someone that always made me feel good about myself when we'd talk. I don't know if she ever really knew that, or if anyone else in my family knew I thought that, because I didn't really show it all that well, or even think to try to. She's the grandmother that I once pushed into the pool at a family reunion to try and get some laughs from my other relatives (and she never knew how to swim). You see, it took me a while to figure out how to show respect. If she were alive nowadays, I'd tell her thanks for saying nice things to me about how I've got a good soul. I mean, I'm not going to go on about that and get all sad—really I'm not sad about it, because I know she knew I was thankful—I'm just trying to give an example about what I've learned about respect.

The reason I originally wanted to write this was to empower women. I think it's more about respect though, isn't it? I still want to do a little women empowerment, so here that goes.

Women are pretty much the same as men, except we have different organs. Besides that, I don't think there's any difference. Women are sexy. Women are humans. Men are humans too. Some women are really pretty awesome. (I mean, *everyone's* pretty awesome in their own way.) Sometimes women are easier to talk to than men. But it depends on the person. Some men are easier to talk to than some women. I guess what I'm saying, is that there's no difference. Women and men are both good. Yeah.

And so I'll conclude all this '*Women*' story by telling you this. The thing that I'd originally set out to accomplish and that landed me in the counselor's office—getting Abby's number—I accomplished successfully. I finished putting her number in my phone when I was under my desk, just after she walked in the door before she made eye contact with me. That was the silver lining about all that. At first I was too embarrassed to do anything with the number such as call her or anything, but then, after about a month went by, I built up the courage to send her the occasional text like, "Hi," or, "Hi Abby." Initially she'd reply, "Who's this?" and then, later in the year, she stopped replying. I had a crush though, I just didn't know what I should say. During class one day, I texted her, "I can see you", intentionally and playfully trying to be creepy. I saw her look down at her phone, then look back up and glance around the room. I held my laugh in and started to text another faux-creepy message. I actually typed, "I like your jeans : )", but, fortunately, I decided against sending that. Instead, I erased it and wrote, "turn around". A second after I sent it, I saw Abby look back down at the phone in her lap, then she looked up, but, she never turned around and looked at me. The humiliation of sitting there the rest of the period, knowing I'd just outed myself as the phantom texter, was enough to make me never text her again. Her number is still in my phone's contacts.

# Lupis and the Erector

*A children's Christmas lesson on having character.*

Had I never found the fifty-dollar bill, my worst day ever wouldn't be the day my cat Lupis ran away, because then he wouldn't have ever run away to begin with. But I did find the fifty-dollar bill, and so he did run away, and that worst day ever came exactly two weeks after last Christmas day—fifty weeks ago, today.

I found the fifty-dollar bill in the kitchen on that Christmas Eve morning. I'd been searching in my mom's purse only for a stick of gum when I came across it. Yes I knew that being there in my mother's purse the bill probably belonged to her, but it wasn't in her wallet, it was just sitting on top of everything as if someone had misplaced it there, so I figured I should take it before someone else did. Part of me felt guilty, but a larger part of me felt so incredibly grateful. I still had to buy my parents Christmas presents, and I had no money—well, no money until I came across the fifty, that is.

I stowed the bill away in my blue-jean pocket and went outside. My mom was on a ladder, putting lights up along the edge of the roof, and I told her I was gonna take a bike ride up to the mall to do a little Christmas shopping.

"Okay Grover," she called down. "Make sure you bring your cell phone with you, and that you're back by six. Grandma and Grampy will be here for supper then."

I said all right and went and got my bike from the garage. I pulled on a pair of ugly red mittens, put my beret on, and pedaled off.

The bitter wind blew sharply across my face. I sang Christmas songs to distract myself from how cold I was. I hit the brakes as I came to a traffic light, my back wheel slid on an ice patch, and I almost fell off the dang bike. *Whew!* That was a close one.

I walked through the mall differently than I'd ever walked through it before. Normally it was just a fun place to go and see interesting things and people, and to eat some nice foods and ask Mom and Dad if I could get a nice toy. But now, with fifty dollars in my pocket, there were new possibilities before me. A store was not just a place to go and stroll around looking longingly at gizmos and gadgets, it was a place where I could walk in, contemplate what I'd like to attain, and then acquire that thing whenever I'd like. I felt a sense of maturity, and power. And since I was searching for gifts for my parents, I felt a bit gracious as well.

For my mom I purchased a twenty-dollar buckskin wallet. And for my dad, I first attempted to buy a nice bottle of wine, but since I was eleven I could not do that, so I searched on and purchased him a handsome velvet shirt and a matching velvet hat.

Outside the mall, shopping bags hanging from my left wrist, I hopped onto my bike and checked the time. *5:53PM*! I pedaled like a madman, straight out of the parking lot, across town, into my neighborhood, and to my house. I threw the bike down, ran to the door, combed my hair, gathered my breath, and then, feeling nice and collected, I rang the doorbell. As I waited for my mom or dad to answer, I lifted my sleeve and glanced at my watch again. 6:00PM. *Excellent.*

Dinner with my parents and grandparents was good. We had stuffed quail and mashed potatoes. My mom played a Frank Sinatra Christmas album. The spirit of the room was as golden as the flames that flickered atop the red wax candles sitting on the table.

"What'd you ask for Grover?" Grampy asked me.

"An erector set, and a cat," I told him.

"An erector set?" he replied, apparently surprised. "Your father had one of those. I didn't even know they still made them."

"Neither did we," my mother said. "But they do—thank heavens."

"I saw it on Sandlot," I told the table. "I want to build a rocket."

"You can't build a rocket with an erector set," Dad said. "Believe me— I've tried."

"Oh yes he has!" Grampy said with a laugh.

"I remember that," Grandma said, laughing as well.

"I haven't heard *this* story…" Mom implored curiously.

"C'mon, tell it!" I shouted.

"Okay, okay," Dad said, and took a sip of wine to get ready for the telling of the story. "So when I was in the fifth grade," he began, "I got an erector set for my birthday. I loved the thing—played with it night and day, anytime I wasn't doing schoolwork. So one day I get this bright idea to build a rocket." Grampy chuckled a bit, probably excited about the climax he knew was coming. "So I make a pretty decent body for the rocket, right? It's got a chassis and all that. So now I just need the engine. 'Okay,' I think, 'what do I need for an engine?' The first thing that comes to mind is a watch—I guess because it's so mechanical or something—and the second thing that comes to mind is firecrackers." Grandma, as if then remembering the climax as well, shook her head in playful shame. "So who do I know that owns a watch? Dad. All right good—got that taken care of. And where will I get the firecrackers? At the stand on Grand street. So that night, while Dad—Grampy—is sleeping, I go into his room and carefully take off his Rolex. I bring it to my room with me and hide it in my drawer. Grampy freaks out the next day because he loves the watch, right?" Grampy nodded in agreement. "I go and buy the fireworks that afternoon. I've got the in-gredients, now I'm ready for the launch. I take everything to the back-yard and set the little erector-rocket on a wooden stump—the launch pad. I attach the watch to the bottom of the rocket with a double-sided magnet, and then I use a rope to tie the fireworks around that. Now, there's tomcats, sparklers, Russian fire cherries... everything. So—I think you can see where this is headed—I take a handful of matches, strike them all at once, light all the wicks, and *run*. Just as I get behind the shed, I hear the fireworks start to go off. *Shpew*! *Fwat*! *Pow*!" He was making firework noises with his mouth and using his hands to show what the explosions looked like. "I peek my head around the corner, hoping to see the rocket flying towards the moon, but all I see is a bunch of fireworks going off like crazy, smoke everywhere, and my rocket crumbling apart..."

"Wow," I said. "What happened to Grampy's watch?"

"Destroyed," Dad replied. "Destroyed."

Grampy wasn't laughing, and Grandma was rubbing his back. The spir-its were still good, but Grampy just must've loved that watch.

"They took up my erector set after that, and I was grounded for a month," Dad said.

"Well can you blame us?" Grandma asked playfully.

"I guess not," Dad said, smiling. "But man, what a lousy thing to happen to a birthday present. I mean, I'm not *blaming* anyone, of course. But then, don't you remember how bad my Christmas presents were that year too?"

"Yeah," Grandma started laughing. "I guess it just wasn't your year!"

Everyone laughed. It was quiet for a moment after the laughing settled, and then mom asked, "Anyone hungry for desert?"

"*Ooh*! Me, me, me!" I screamed.

"Settle down *Grover*," she said back in an unexpectedly stern tone that shut me right up. I was not the only one surprised at her tone, and she could see this by the expressions on our faces, and she said, "Oh, I'm sorry. I'm sorry Grover. I was just thinking about something bad that happened. It's not so bad—so don't worry. I'll go get the cobbler and then I'll tell you guys about it. Sorry. I'll be right back."

She disappeared into the kitchen and came back in a moment later with a peach cobbler in each hand. She set them on the table and everyone dug in. It was scrumptious. I felt no grudge at her for snapping at me, and everyone else's spirits were still golden as well.

"Anyways, what had happened is," my mom started. "When I went to the Salvation Army to give them the donation for the sponsor kid, I looked in my purse, and my money—the fifty-dollars—was gone."

I froze in my boots. Shivers icily tickled my skin and gave me goose bumps.

"Oh no," Grandma said.

"And I know it was in there this morning. I placed it right on top of everything so I wouldn't forget to go donate it."

I started to choke on my spoon and pulled it out of my mouth. I was fine but kept on coughing, hoping this would change the subject, and after my dad hit me on the back a few times I spit the cobbler out of my mouth as if I were done choking. When they saw that I was all right though, they continued the conversation.

"I had stopped at the gas station to fill up on the way to the Salvation Army, and the only thing I can think is that maybe the criminal snuck into the car and took the money while I was out pumping the gas."

"Yeah," Dad said, shaking his head. "That'd be it. Godd*mnit. What a shame."

Mom looked as if she was about to cry. I felt like splinters were being pushed into every part of my body. But I didn't say a thing.

"Well let's not let this ruin Christmas," Grandma said. "Let's dance."

We danced and had a very nice time. Everyone completely forgot about the fifty. Every once in a while throughout the evening it'd flash into my mind for a moment and I'd feel a cramp rise in my abdomen, but then I'd get caught up in the fun of the night and forget about it. When Grandma and Grampy left, I went to my room, wrapped up the presents I'd purchased, and then set them under the tree in the living room, feeling a slight bit of that guilt as I did so, but also enough generosity to blur it right out. And as I lay in bed that night, I thought only about Santa—wondering where he was at that moment, imagining him walking through our hall, to the tree, lying down the presents, and thanking the heavens that I lived in a world where such a saint existed. I woke up at 6:21AM, hopped out of bed, stripped out of my pajamas, marched to my parent's room, and excitedly shook them out of bed. They were a little drowsy, so I went to the kitchen and fixed them a pot of coffee, being careful not to look in the direction of the living room, since I knew my parents would want to see my face and the glorious expression that'd be on it when I first saw the presents. They thanked me for the coffee, my mom got her camera, and, with my mom filming my face, we proceeded together to the living room.

There it was. A nice stack of presents. "Oh nice!" I yelled, and jumped over to the stack, my parents laughing at my excitement.

I searched for which one I wanted to open first. There were eight presents total, all labeled 'To: Grover', and six of these said 'From: Santa'. The other two, the two largest ones, were labeled 'From: Mom and Dad'. I picked up the second-largest one.

"Nice!" I said as I hefted it up onto my shoulder. "Can I open this one?"

"Knock yourself out," Dad said. "That one's from us."

I tore into the paper and threw the shreds over my shoulder. "YES! YES! An erector set!"

My mom smiled from behind the camera, and my dad winked and sipped his coffee.

"Thank you!" I said as I rubbed the cardboard box, imagining what I'd build first. Then I asked, "Can I open the other one?"

"Which other one?" Dad asked, though he knew exactly which other one.

"The big one," I said, pointing.

"I don't know. Can he open that one now, Honey?" he asked Mom.

"Yeah. I think he can."

I slowly approached the present. The wrapping paper was blue and had pictures of angels on it. I had a feeling that I knew what was inside. I felt like there might be something living in there. I put my hand on the top of the present. I carefully ripped off a strand of wrapping paper. The box below was white. I ripped off another strand, revealing another bit of white box. This bit had a hole in it though. *A breathing hole*? I looked to my mom and dad. They smiled at me. I knew what it was. It was a cat.

And what a beautiful cat it was. Green eyes and orange fur. I still remember first holding Lupis in my arms. I unwrapped the box and he jumped right up into them, purring like he already knew I was his daddy. "Lupis," I said to my parents as a tear rolled down my cheek. "I'll call him Lupis."

I was almost too woozy with delight to carry on opening the presents after that. We took a five-minute break so I could lie on my back and catch my senses, as Lupis crawled around me, examining his new owner and environment. It was heaven. And when I came back to, and remembered that I still had all of Santa's gifts to open, I sat up and went back to the pile, Lupis by my side.

I picked out the smallest present first. I removed the wrapping paper, opened the box, and found a little ball of cloth. I took the cloth out and saw that it was a balled-up pair of socks.

"That's an unusual present," I said to my mom and dad. They laughed.

"Sure is," Mom agreed.

I laughed too. I didn't mind at all. I was too happy with what I'd received already to be disappointed over a single lousy gift.

Next I picked out the biggest of Santa's presents. I unwrapped it and found a plain white cotton sweater.

"White like snow," I said, not letting this get me down either.

The next present was a pair gloves. They were nice enough, better than the ugly mittens I owned, but I did wonder why all of Santa's gifts so far had been articles of clothing. My parents thought it was a little curious too.

When I unwrapped the next one and found that it was underwear, I turned to my parents and asked, "Is this a *joke*?"

"No," my dad said. "So strange."

"It is odd," my mom added.

I pet Lupis a bit to calm myself down before opening the next one. It was a pair of jeans. I felt tears welling up behind my eyes. My mom went and got me one of the leftover cookies that we'd laid out for Santa, and as I chewed it my sadness mellowed some, and my dad spoke a few encouraging words, helping me come to terms with the fact that I might not be receiving anything excellent from Santa this year.

I opened the last present and was neither surprised nor disappointed to find a black-leather belt. Santa had given me an outfit, which was just so odd. He'd always given me the best presents in the past. The best. Things I hadn't asked for or even thought to ask for. And it's not that I minded receiving clothes for gifts—I mean, I *liked* clothes—but the outfit wasn't even my style. It was odd, and somewhat devastating.

My parents and I sat in the living room for a bit, processing what had gone down. Eventually though, as I pet Lupis and we talked about this and that, we all forgot about the gifts and just started enjoying Christmas morning. Besides, I'd received everything I wanted, Lupis and the erector. We had some pancakes, did a little caroling, and then Grandma and Grampy and the rest of the family came over, and we had a really nice time.

The next day I tried out my erector set. It was pretty sweet and I was able to build a cool little track to roll my marbles on. I spent a couple weeks building and trying out different tracks, and enjoyed it quite a bit. My time with Lupis during these weeks was unforgettable. I had this little fake rat, and I'd always dangle it by the tail in front of him and let him swat at it, just for hours. And even though he was a cat, I got a leash and would take him for walks. One day I walked with him across the bridge, over to the creek, and we went fishing—me with a pole, Lupis with his paws. Guess who caught something first. Lupis. We had fish for dinner that night.

It was getting towards the second week of January when my mom decided to take the Christmas tree down. That day at school, I had decided I'd stop with the marble tracks and start with the rocket that I'd originally wanted to build. When I got home, I said hi to my mom, who was there in the living room dismantling the tree. (We had an artificial tree.) She said hi back, and I went to my room to get Lupis and the erector set.

I went to the backyard with Lupis and the erector, tied Lupis's leash to the tree, and began to build beside him. I held the erector pieces up in different ways, contemplating the best design for the rocket.

"What do you think Lupy?" I asked him.

*Meow.*

I ruffled his fur and kissed his wet little nose.

I tried out another design.

"Is that better?"

*Meow.*

"Oh you liked the last one better? Me too, baby. Me too."

I began to construct the rocket. It was a process of much trial and error. But it was fun. I constructed the bottom, and had just started working on the middle when I heard a *meow*.

I turned to Lupis. He was walking back and forth, a little restlessly. He sat down and scratched at his collar.

*Meow.*

I pet his head and turned back to the rocket.

*Meow.*

"Lupis, *what?*" I was surprised at the irritability in my tone.

He was nibbling at the leash.

"What is it Lupis?" I asked, more friendlily.

*Meow.* He was scratching at the tree and nibbling and pawing at the leash. Something about the tree was bothering him, and I could tell he wanted to roam the yard. I always let him roam the yard, but only when I was just lounging around back there with him. I figured I could take a break from focusing on the rocket to lounge with Lupis for a bit.

I unhooked his leash and tickled him a little. He batted my hand away playfully. I tickled him on his stomach and under his neck. I could tell he was laughing inside. I ruffled his hair and wrestled with him. I accidently stepped on his paw and he yelped.

"I'm sorry Lupy!" I said.

*Meow.*

I laid on my back in the grass and he crawled up onto my stomach. He licked my nose, then I laid out my arm and he rolled sideways onto it. We laid there together, his body resting on my arm, looking up at the clouds, and thinking about the future. Lupis was a good cat.

I heard the back door open and turned to see my mother standing there.

"Grover," she said. "Did you get this present for Dad?"

*Huh?* I thought.

Then I looked at what she was holding—the Christmas present for dad that I'd placed under the tree—and remembered that I'd never given my parents their gifts.

"Oh my gosh!" I said. "Yeah I did. I got one for you too."

"Oh really?" she said. "I found this one for dad—it says it's from you—and I found one for me that's from Santa."

"Really?"

"Yeah. Come look."

I went with her to the living room, where the tree was now fully dismantled and almost completely boxed away, and saw the other present—the one for Mom—there on the ground.

"Yep. Those are them," I told her.

"I found them just as I was finishing boxing the tree."

"Oh, this is awesome! You guys can open them right now."

"Okay. Go get Dad."

I ran to my dad's office and told him to come to the living room for a surprise. He came, and me and Mom explained about the presents.

"Why does mine say 'from Santa', though?" Mom asked after she finished with her bit of the story.

"Oh... I don't know actually. I must've just written it wrong, because I was pretty tired when I wrapped them."

Dad opened his first. "Oh I love it!" he exclaimed as he held the velvet shirt up to his chest to see if it'd fit. "And a perfect fit too." He put the velvet hat on his head, then came over and hugged me. "I'm so excited to wear this out in public," he said. "And what kind of material is this?"

"It's pure velvet," I replied proudly.

"Oh it is?" I detected a shift in his emotions. Maybe a slight bit of concern. "Hmm," he said. "I'm allergic to velvet."

He took the hat off and placed it on the table with the shirt. "I'm sorry buddy. I love it, but I can't wear it."

I tried to smile. "It's okay, Dad. I'm glad you liked it."

"Can I open mine?" Mom asked.

"Yeah," I said, my mood brightening a little. "Go ahead."

She picked it up, removed the wrapping paper, and looked at the buckskin wallet. "Beautiful," she said. "Really. Beautiful. I love it."

I smiled and we hugged. She looked back down to admire and inspect the wallet further, flipping it in her hands and rubbing her thumb across the leather. I could tell she really did like it. I watched as she opened the wallet, and I was about to ask if we could maybe go get something to eat, but she said, "Oh, and there's more."

She pulled two sheets of paper from the wallet's main pocket. I could not remember placing them there. That is because I hadn't.

"The Salvation Army?" she said. She made a face at the paper and then turned it towards me. "Why'd you put this in there?"

I looked at the paper. There was a Salvation Army watermark on top, and below it a sort of hand-written list.

"Um... I don't know," I said.

She put the list aside and then looked at the next sheet. Her eyes grew wide as they read whatever was written there.

"It's for you..." she told me. "From Santa."

She handed me the paper, with her finger pointing at the bottom, where Santa had signed his name in purple ink. I read the message that'd been written with the same pen.

*Dear Grover,*
*In your heart you know what is right,*
*I have righted what you wronged tonight,*
*If you are unsure of what I mean then wait a fortnight,*
*Then the tree will turn your darkness into light.*
*Yours truly,*
*Santa*

My hands were trembling. I could not look up at either of my parents. I folded the letter carefully in half and placed it in my back pocket. I stared straight down, at my shoes.

"Grover," my dad asked. "What does it say."

After a moment, I looked back up, but I could not speak. My mom was reading the Salvation Army letter.

"This list," she said. "It's the one from the Christmas child we were supposed to sponsor."

"What?" my dad asked.

"Oh my God," she said. "Oh my God. Grover. What did you do with the clothes you got for Christmas?"

"They're in my closet."

I was scared. Something big was happening, I did not understand what, and I was scared.

"Grover," she began. "What does your letter mean?"

I could not tell her. I had a notion, but I could not let them know what I'd done.

She handed the list to Dad. "This is what our Christmas sponsor child asked for..."

He read the list. When he finished, he looked up at me, then over at Mom.

"What did he ask for?" I asked. "What's going on?"

Dad handed me the list. I read.

*Dear sponsor,*

*Thank you so much, I have never received presents before. I am an orphan and you don't know how much this means to me. My school year will be starting at the beginning of January, and I really need this for school, because it's mandatory.*

*Thank you, much love, and a merry Christmas!*
*Roger*

*List:*
*One pair of socks*
*One pair of blue jeans*
*One black belt*

*One pair of briefs*
*One white sweater*
*One pair of gloves*
*One velvet shirt*
*And one velvet hat*

"I... I don't know what to say," I said to my parents, voice quivering as I spoke.

"What did the letter say? The one from Santa," Dad asked, his voice calm and curious.

I felt ashamed. I'd really screwed up. Really bad. This poor guy Roger hadn't gotten his clothes in time for school because of my dishonesty. I'd always known that Santa was always watching me, I'd heard that before, but I figured that maybe since he too could see that the money I'd stolen, the fifty-dollar bill, was just sitting there in the purse when I'd found it, out of the wallet, right on top of everything, maybe he wouldn't be able to blame me, maybe he'd think I really had thought it'd been misplaced and then taken it innocently enough. This is just what I'd hoped he'd think though, all those days ago when I took it. But now I realized that this was not the case. I could not trick him. Santa knew what I was thinking. Always. I'd known it was my mom's money right from the beginning. How foolish I'd been. I felt like such a dead-beat. I began to cry.

"I took the fifty-dollars," I said to my parents. "That's how I bought your presents."

They didn't know what to say.

"I'm such an idiot." I sniffled. "I'm the biggest idiot in the world."

Dad placed his hand on my shoulder. "Grover," he began. "Grover, look at me."

I looked up into his eyes. They were swimming with mercy, and had a comforting effect on me. He wiped a tear from my cheek. "Everyone makes mistakes."

I cried harder. "I'm sorry."

Mom placed her hand on my other shoulder, the left one. "It's all right Grover. You're eleven, and you'll learn from your mistakes."

Then she said, "Grover. Show Dad the letter Santa wrote you."

I reached into my pocket and nervously handed it to my dad. He read through it and said, "Hmm..."

Then, after a moment of thought, he smiled. Mom smiled too.

"He's righted your wrong Grover," Dad said. "That's why he gave us the outfit. He wants us to give it to Roger. You have nothing to worry about. Nothing at all. He's not holding it against you."

"We aren't either," Mom added.

"But Roger's year already started," I said. "He couldn't go to school since he didn't have his outfit in time. Ah, I *hate* myself!"

Dad squeezed my right shoulder reassuringly, and Mom squeezed the left. "You know what?" Mom said. "Roger sent this letter from Ottawa. I just read this morning that their school year got pushed back a week due to the snow storms."

She laughed and so did my dad.

"Wow..." Dad said, smiling as he shook his head in disbelief. "Wow..."

At first I did not understand what they were so smiley about. Then it dawned on me. Roger's school hadn't started its year yet. He'd get the outfit right on time. Santa *had* righted my wrong. He'd *completely* righted it. My darkness began to leave, and in came the light. I smiled. My parents smiled widely back.

"Okay," Mom said, and picked the last few artificial branches up off the ground. "I'm just going to drag the box out to the garage, and then we can figure out tonight's dinner plans." She brought the branches over to the box, and the moment she dropped them inside with the rest of the tree, I heard a sound come from the backyard, and knew that something was bugging me.

*Lupis.*

"Oh God, I left him outside!"

I scrammed out of the living room. I heard my parents call "*What?*" from behind me as I ran, but I was already out of there. I went straight through the kitchen, flung open the back door, and then froze.

My parents were soon right there behind me, and when they looked into the backyard, they froze as well.

Our tree lay sideways through the middle of the yard. It was the tree that Lupis had been tied to. It'd collapsed. I could see neither Lupis nor my erector set, which had sat right where the tree now lay.

"*Looopis!*" I screamed.

I stumbled down the back steps into the yard. I went to the tree and pushed the branches aside as I made my way to the spot where I had last laid with Lupis. The erector was there. Crushed. "Oh gosh." I turned to my parents. Dad had his arm around Mom, and they both wore looks of deep concern.

"Don't just stand there you guys! Don't just stand there! Lupis is gone! He might be dea—" I couldn't say it. I couldn't begin to fathom the possibility that the tree had crushed Lupis. I broke down, dropped to my knees, and began to sob. My parents came to my side, grabbed me beneath each arm, and walked me inside...

That was the worst day of my life. When the maintenance men came and took the tree away a week later, we could find no sign of Lupis. This was the good news. Lupis was still alive. The bad news was that I'd never see him again, because he'd run away and would never find his way back—forever wandering, lost, starved, and alone. Also my other main present had been crushed beyond repair. My parents did send Roger his outfit that night when I lost Lupis, so that was nice to know, but my soul still felt just as crushed as the erector, and like the erector, nothing anyone did could salvage it. I did my best to be a good person and not to steal anymore, and after a few months I came out of this despair, but I never fully did get over the loss of the little guy. The thing is though, I can't say I've really been given a chance to fully get over the loss. I say that because, this morning—Christmas morning—exactly fifty weeks after the loss, Lupis was found. He was found by me, in a box that was labeled 'From: Santa', beneath the Christmas tree.

Diary Entry 3/7/13

I took the train into San Luis Obispo yesterday and got in around
3:30PM. And then, at night, as I walked through the shopping centre
towards Barnes and Noble, I looked briefly into a storefront window
and saw a man—either a bi-sexual or an employee—grabbing a male
mannequin's crotch. I just walked on. I spent a couple hours reading in
the bookstore, and when I left and walked out and back through the
shopping centre, I looked again into that store window, and this time
the man was struggling to squeeze his way between a few female
mannequins. This made me realize that he wasn't a pervert or anything, but just an employee adjusting the mannequins. I came to this
conclusion, because I thought that if he weren't an employee, surely he
wouldn't have been able to get away with two hours of that mannequin groping, right there in the window, without a manager or employee saying something.
This morning a girl recognized me at the hostel. It was her birthday
and she knew me from YouTube. I went to the library and spent five
hours typing a 5,200 word story called Lupis and the Erector. It fell out
of my fingers. They just danced around the keyboard and the story
filled the Word document like a flood. When the library closed at five, I
went and ate at Natural Café, and a girl named Stephanie recognized
me there. Then I went to this other café after I finished eating, and had
tea as I re-wrote some of the story. I was there for about two or three
hours, and some guy recognized me, and then a group of three girls
recognized me, and one of them barked like a dog to impress me, because they wanted to impress me to be my friend for some reason, but
I was not impressed (they were all very nice though). Then, at the
same café, another group of girls recognized me. That's the most I've
been recognized. I think because it's a college town. Life is weird.
(P.S. Update from the next day: this morning a girl recognized me at a
place called Sally Loo's when I went to get breakfast, and I ate breakfast with her, her parents, and her three friends. And then I got recognized at a café at nighttime.)

Diary entry 3/12/13

I got news that they went another direction on How to Catch a Monster. I'm still really glad I got the chance to do those auditions though. Really thankful. Time to write and travel and find something else.

All the orange, colored like rust, deep and crevice-y—the Grand Canyon is beautiful upon first sight. And as I hiked in, as I went deeper, the truth was revealed. It was the beauty that drew me into this trap where the sun almost killed me. A lack of knowledge had been given to me, and I did not realize as I travelled farther and farther down, that I'd have to climb farther and farther back out. Beauty is in the small things, and anything big is good for a quick sight, but is ultimately deadly.

I escaped because of kindness. Halfway back up out of the canyon, liquids drunk long ago—back at my turn around point—I stood leaning against a rock, lips parched, skin burned, on the verge of total collapse—system failure. And then came the man in brown clothes. Red-bearded face, probably thirty.

"Are you all right? Do you need something to drink?"

I spit the peanuts from my mouth. "Yes... Please."

He removed the Camelpack from his back as he approached me.

"Here you go. There's Gatorade in here," he said, handing me the tube stemming from the pack.

I sucked on the tube and my mouth was filled with wet energy. I swallowed the energy, and the electrolytes dissolved into my bloodstream, pumped through to my brain, and I became halfway solid again. After a few gulps I looked to the man and said, "Thank you."

"No problem at all. Gotta stay hydrated—especially in those corduroys. Will you be all right going up?"

I nodded. "Of course."

"Okay... You got a bottle? I can pour you some of this."

He filled my empty water bottle about halfway with the yellow Gatorade, and before turning to go he said, "Have a good day."

"Ditto," I told him, to save time.

The Gatorade was gone within a half mile. But I reached the top, struggle it might have been, and laid there in the dirt on my back, looking at the sky, conqueror and conqueree.

The beauty had betrayed me. Here I was back at the top, where she'd first filled me with wonder. And now, four hours later, was I better than I was then? Not yet. Eventually I would learn a lesson from the mistake I'd made—the mistake of being drawn in—but at that moment I was just another piece of trash beaten and bruised and strewn about by that tricky mother Nature.

The lesson that made me better for it was realized recently, as I sat and thought about the ways of the world. The beauty of that big canyon was good on first glance, but as I went deeper, the truth was revealed. I think I said that already. But it is what I learned. The counterpart to that statement is this: Beauty is in the small things—*true* beauty, that is.

The world is a murderous place—a murderous place. But it is also a place of life. You will find that life in a blade of grass. There is no murder there. The murder is in the ocean. The murder is in the canyon. The murder is in the animals.

And where do humans fit in?

I catch a falling leaf any time I see one. If I am walking under a tree and the breeze blows one loose, I leap and I catch it in my hand. Every time. I do this because I believe in metaphors. This metaphor reveals the way of the world for us humans. This world's been spinning for years and years and years. Eventually that tree that I'm walking under sprouted out from under the Earth's dirt, then it grew and grew—it's probably at least a twenty or thirty or forty year old tree, since it's bigger than me and covered in leaves. So then, I was born onto this Earth back in 1991. I lived all my life, and now I'm in this city for whatever reason, walking down this street for whatever reason, and the wind blows right now, pulling a leaf loose from this tree older than me, and I'm there to catch it, out of all the places in the world I could've been. And so it is with luck, and with unluckiness, and all that stuff. When my YouTube video got 50,000 views over night and my life kind of changed, it was just a falling leaf. Or when my baseball bat ricocheted off the basketball hoop pole and smacked my head open (later sewn shut by thirteen stitches), it was just another leaf.

So that is the way of the world. It is good to think about these metaphors.

(I'm so flexible that if I stand up, lock my legs at the knees, and bend forward from the waist with my arms extended, I can not only touch my toes, but can lay my hands out completely flat on the ground. I got this way because as a senior I spent ten seconds every day leaning forward and reaching for my toes. Just ten seconds, but every day. At the beginning of the year it was a struggle to reach my foot, and at the end I could lay my hands flat there for a minute, and could also most nearly do the Chinese splits. There's a metaphor.)

## The End
(Written April 21st, 2013.)

A memoir is the story of a person's life. The natural end to the story of any person's life is their death. But since I am writing my own memoir, I have to come up with a different ending, because I prefer for it to be released before my death. I cannot know the exact details of what will happen over the course of the rest of my life, but what I do know—and what I want to share with you, as an ending to this book—is how I plan to go about the rest of my life. This plan is a promise to myself and to you.

I promise to be a wholesome man. Loving of my family. Good and honest. Simple and pure. Wise. Mighty. Loyal friend. I will get married to a sweet woman, and we will live life together and do crazy things. I promise.

## One Last Thing

That was a good ending, but I realized something quite important a few days ago, wrote it down in my diary, and wanted to share it here with you.

So, here is that diary entry:

*6/4 [2013]*

*Me and mom went to a local play yesterday. I had a good time. Honestly very good.*

*I was a little worried about myself this morning, thinking about how I never dance or sing or let loose.*

*What I was just thinking though, was that I'm always thinking of advice I could offer other people, or about what other people need. And then I thought that it could be very valuable to step outside of my body for a minute, and to think what advice I'd offer myself if I weren't myself. What advice would I offer this twenty-one year old human (me)?*

- *Do push ups and sit ups every other day (at least 100), since it's good for your physique/body/health and makes you feel good.*
- *Don't be afraid to embarrass yourself. What's worse, people not liking you because they don't like who you are/how you act, or people not knowing you (and hereby not having a chance to like you) because you hide yourself away? I think the second one is worse. It's better to risk humiliation and rejection, because if you do there's a chance for greatness to come into your life, and if you don't, if you hide yourself away, then you don't give those people that'd like you the chance to like you, and you're kind of the walking dead. So please let loose.*
- *Don't think bitterly.*
- *Appreciate your blessings and skills and good qualities.*
- *Understand and remember that life is 1000x more important than art.*
- *Enjoy your talents, and share them with others.*
- *See the best in and appreciate your family members.*

*(That's good. I'll focus on these for now.)*

# Timothy of the Library

[First entry written on June 18, 2013.]

Timothy pulled the magazine from the shelf, opened it, and flipped through the pages until something caught his eye. A rich looking pasta dish apparently covered in pesto sauce. He rubbed his finger in little circles over the surface of the page. He pretended to pick one of the noodles up out of the page, and then he let his head fall back as he held the invisible noodle above his mouth and dropped it in. As he chewed it he observed beautiful eggshell paint of the library ceiling above. Flawless. If he had to describe it in a word, he would describe the ceiling with the word flawless. But if given the opportunity to use more than one word, he would have said, "That paint was a flawless choice. I've loved eggshell paint ever since I subletted this beautiful one bedroom house back in LA a little over a year ago. If I have a house, that's the paint I'll use on its interior."

He looked down from the ceiling and out the window at the passing cars. Tim was at the library solely because he could think of nowhere else to be. A pool would be nice on this summer day, but he already went swimming this morning.

He left the reading room and went to the Teen Zone—the area of the library that had teen books. (Tim isn't the one who dubbed it the Teen Zone. There was a big sign that said it.) In the Teen Zone he approached a shelf of books, placed his pointer finger on one of the books' spine, slid his finger down the row of books, and then pulled from the shelf the book his finger had come to a rest on. He took a seat in one of the cushioned chairs and opened the book. It was written by an author named Avi, and after the first two pages had failed to engage his interest, he began to scan through the book, reading a paragraph here and there, and eventually realizing that it'd been written by a coward—someone not brave enough to express whatever was actually lingering in their adult heart.

Tim was a writer too, and that's why he was able to observe these kinds of things.

He put the book on the table and then started back towards the reading room. An Indian man entered the room just before him and held the door open as he stepped inside. Tim thanked him, and when the

Indian man turned, Tim observed that he was wearing a quite flaw-lessly tucked-in linen shirt. Tim was wearing a linen long-sleeve too, though his was blue and not khaki. He momentarily considered reach-ing out and touching the Indian man's top, knowing that if he could manage to rub it in-between his fingers for only a second he'd immedi-ately be able to recognize whether or not it was linen, but he decided against doing this because people get suspicious and it really wasn't that important.

Tim stepped over to the desk on which his laptop still sat, took a seat, and opened a word document. He wondered what he should write about. He wanted to write something because he could think of noth-ing better to do, and also because it was his destiny to be a writer. He looked at the wall beside him and then he thought, "I'll just write about what I know," and then he started writing this story. I am Tim. (But, in case you were unable to infer this, that's just a pseudo-name.)

Lolo Jones is cute.

Shortly before typing this, Timothy had leaned back in the wooden chair and pondered what he should write about. He opened the Word document that contained a list of story titles for his stories he'd not yet written about, and when he saw the words **San Francisco convention** written in regular Cambria font like this: San Francisco convention, he decided that that was what he'd like to write about, and that he'd like to do it in the third person. After deciding that this is what he'd do, he rubbed his temples as if he had a headache, which he did not, and then he procrastinated by going online and checking his e-mails, seeing in his peripherals a photo of Lolo Jones on his e-mail page with some headline underneath it. He admired the woman's face, and then he closed his Internet because he had no e-mails. He attempted to get his writing juices flowing by typing this paragraph, and then he decided that after he wrote this sentence he'd go to the bathroom and then start on the San Francisco convention story upon his return.

He rose from his chair and turned to look at the boy with the turquoise shirt and spiky black hair sitting behind him. He observed him for three seconds and deemed him trustworthy enough to watch his laptop.

"Would you mind watching my laptop if I just go to the bathroom for a second?" Timothy asked.

"Yeah, sure," the boy said, giving a brief thumbs up.

Timothy exited the reading room and ran his hands through his hair as he made his way across the library. The red-headed librarian behind the desk was cute, but he didn't know if she was sixteen or twenty-two. She could have been anywhere in-between, so he stopped at the desk, hoping to find out where exactly in that age range she lay.

"Do you have any books that are… biographies?"

"Biographies?"

Timothy nodded.

"Yes, they're in the nonfiction section," the girl said as she began to rise from her chair. "Let me show you."

"Actually I have to go to the bathroom. But I'll just ask you when I come back."

"Okay."

He turned, walked coolly through the automatic doors that opened into the lobby, got a quick drink from the water fountain, glanced through the lobby window at the girl as he walked towards the bathroom door, and then entered the bathroom.

He went to a urinal, did what you do there, and then went to the sink.

He stared into the mirror as he washed his hands, and felt very glad that he'd chosen to wear his khaki linen pants and his red and white striped top today. As he pushed his hair off of his forehead and into place, his eyes drifted down to the blemish on the left side of his chin. Blemishes had been a struggle with Timothy ever since the age of thirteen, so he didn't really mind it all that much since he'd learned by now that there was nothing that could be done about it. There was also a blemish right on the inside of his nose up by his left eyebrow, and another one under his left cheekbone near the sideburn. The right side of his face was the good side of his face today, and with this knowledge and a neatly organized head of hair he exited the bathroom ready to talk to the red-headed girl.

"Okay," she said, standing as he approached the desk.

Timothy followed her to the non-fiction section, observing her hair as he walked behind her. She wore it in curls that Tim could tell she'd done with a straightener. (He was able to recognize this because his mom sometimes used this technique too.) It was pretty hair, but he observed it only with curiosity, not desire, since he did not yet know her age.

Having showed Timothy to the bookshelf with the biographies, the girl turned to leave, but as she did, Timothy asked, "Are any of these required reading at your college?"

"Uh-uh," the girl answered, shaking her head and turning back around to face him.

"Oh... What about for high school?"

"No. I don't know."

She smiled politely and Timothy nodded, angling his body slightly to the left so that her view would favor the right side of his face. He really

132

wasn't so intensely interested in the girl, it's just that at this point he was pretty curious what her age was, and he was very curious to find out if he was a good enough detective to find out. (He was not a detective, but that's the word he would have used to describe the way he felt in that situation. For example, to make this point clear, if someone would have asked how he felt standing there asking that girl those questions, he would have said, "Kind of detective-ish. But only in a fun way.") Also, he was enjoying the girl's company.

"Well, what's a book that they require you to read at your college?"

"Uh... they had us read Things Fall Apart in my English class."

"Oh," he said, nodding and knowing that he'd make a decent 'detective'. And since the girl was fair game, and also very sweet and nice to talk to (and a librarian/librarian's assistant on top of that), he attempted to continue the conversation.

"Was that pretty good?"

"Yeah, I enjoyed it."

He was going to say, "I never liked reading until I finished high school," but she was starting to back away, and, recognizing that she probably needed to get back to work, he played it cool and said, "Yeah, I know what that's like. See ya," and he went back to the reading room.

He took a seat at the desk and looked at his laptop, which reminded him that the boy with the spiked hair had been watching it that whole time. He turned to the boy and said, "Thanks for watching it. I'm sorry, I wasn't in the bathroom that whole time, I just forgot and was looking at books."

"Oh, it's all right," the boy said with no sign of agitation. He looked at Timothy a moment longer, and then added, "And I don't mean to bother you, but you were great in 21 Jump Street."

"Oh thank you," Timothy whispered back immediately, before swiveling around in his chair and staring into the sleeping computer screen.

For a moment there was an anxiety in Timothy's mind. His thoughts were something like, "If he recognizes me, and he was watching my laptop, maybe he went on my computer and checked my e-mails and even sent a few e-mails out to some of my higher-profile contacts and blemished my reputation." But these thoughts and the anxiety that came with them were gone as quickly as they came. Timothy could tell by the way the boy had said, "I don't mean to bother you," that he was a level-headed boy with a beautiful heart. He turned in his chair, pretending to stretch his back, and looked at the boy for a couple seconds. The boy was working away on his laptop, not at all fawning over Timothy's presence in the reading room. Timothy turned back in his chair, perfectly at ease, and wiggled his finger around the mouse pad, waking the laptop from its slumber.

He spent about thirty minutes typing all of this (with the exception of the first paragraph, which he'd written before his trip to the bathroom), and after those thirty minutes of writing he decided that he oughtta take a quick little break before getting started on that third person account of his time working at that San Francisco convention (which he did back in 2010).

So he went and got another drink of water. It was an uneventful drink of water; or, at least not eventful enough to delay his writing about the San Francisco convention any longer.

Timothy thought about how to approach the writing of the San Francisco convention story, and then, after typing this sentence, he pressed the 'enter' key two times and began.


### San Francisco Convention

When Timothy was eighteen he was cast in a movie called Project X. He worked for about two months on it, and by the time he was finished he had about $35,000 in his bank account (almost half of which had come from the YouTube videos he'd made throughout high school). He could think of nothing better to do with his time and money, so he decided to travel, hoping to experience new experiences and to be exposed to enlightening and previously unknown aspects of life.

The first destination he would travel to was San Francisco. It was December and he was now nineteen. During the four-week trip he lodged in hostels. It was a trip of great discovery. He often walked the hilly streets just waiting for something to happen, which led to conversations with various hobos (These conversations never really went anywhere past the point of Timothy rejecting, or occasionally appeasing, their request for money.), a sighting of a beautiful bird with gold trim on its wings (known as the...?), and a sighting of the actor James Franco walking in a raincoat on the opposite side of the road. He discovered beatniks at the beatnik museum near City Lights bookstore, and one night he walked into a hotel that he wasn't even staying at, rode the elevator to the top floor, and took a look out the window at the beautiful Union Square.

After two weeks in San Fran he decided to try to do something he'd always wanted to do but had never done before: get an average job.

He went on craigslist and replied to a million ads. Very few responded. Two days after sending out his replies, while perusing around a Border's bookstore right off of Union Square, he felt a vibration against his leg. He reached into his pocket and extracted from it his ringing phone. He answered it, and to his great surprise it was a man working for a company that was holding some convention at the Moscone Center. Even though Timothy had no qualifications, through conversing with the man, the gusto that Timothy had within (as well as his complete availability during the dates of the convention) became so apparent to the man on the other side of the phone that he offered him the job right then and there. He was to work for five days at the Moscone Center, starting the next day.

That is all that Timothy typed of the convention story before remembering that he'd already tried writing about it once before and that it had gone just about the same way: he'd written everything leading up to the point where the convention actually starts, and then realized that he didn't want to write about a d*mn convention at the moment, even if it had been an interesting experience. That was okay though, because he'd written all this (Timothy of the Library II), and he knew that he'd write the rest of that convention story someday (maybe tomorrow?).

"Excuse me. Sorry. I just lost my car key, um…"

The white haired man with the khaki Bermuda shorts looked through his eyeglasses with reservation.

Timothy continued, "I was sitting in that chair earlier and I wanted to check if it's there."

Registering what exactly Timothy's predicament was, the white haired man rose from his chair and said, "Good luck."

Timothy said thanks, set his laptop case on the ground, lowered himself to his knees, and used his fingers to explore the crevices between the cushions of the chair. He felt no signs of any key, so he stood and pulled the seat cushion completely free from the chair. There was nothing beneath it except for the wrapper of a jumbo candy bar.

"Nope," Timothy informed the on-looking white-haired man. He observed the thinness of the legs that extended from beneath the Bermuda shorts, and then looked the man in the eyes and asked, "Did you see a key? It's a Honda key."

"No, I did not," the man answered, shaking his head.

Timothy could tell the man was being honest, so he smiled at him, lifted his laptop case and strapped it over his shoulder, and then left the reading room.

He'd just spent about an hour and a half unsuccessfully trying to type something interesting in that cushioned chair, and had only discovered the absence of the key after deciding that he'd go to the other library to see if he'd have any more luck there, standing from his chair, leaving the reading room, and reaching into an empty left pocket.

Upon discovering the absence he'd gone to the front desk and asked the woman librarian if anyone had turned in a key. She said that someone gave her a USB drive, but no key. He thanked her and decided to go check the other chair he'd sat in that morning—the cushioned one in the back of the library near the biographies.

Before he reached the biography section, Timothy had an idea and stopped walking. He pulled his phone from his pocket, flipped through a few screens, and pulled up the recorder tool. He would record the conversation so that he could later write about it with record accuracy in a Word document, and his writer's block would be relieved. It was a great idea. He pressed record, returned the phone to his pocket, and proceeded to that cushioned chair in the back.

In the chair sat a twenty-something bald man with a handsome face. He lounged in the chair with his legs crossed (right ankle over left knee) and a laptop on his lap. When Timothy approached him he did not look up. Maybe it was because Timothy was standing three feet away and the man was unsure of whether or not Tim was waiting for him to look up, or maybe it was because the man was in a bad mood. Tim did not know, but what he did know was that either way it might make for good writing material.

So Tim leaned forward and waved his hands about a foot from the man's face. The man blinked and looked lazily up towards Timothy.

"Um..." Timothy said.

The man removed the headphones from his ears and Timothy continued.

"I lost my car key, and I was sitting in this chair earlier, and I wanted to see if I could—"

"Is that it?" the man interrupted, pointing to Timothy's key lying on the nearby windowsill.

"Yeah," Tim said with a nod. "Thanks."

The man handed Tim the key, and before he put his headphones back on his head, Tim had to know, "Was it there when you sat here? Or—"

"No, it was on the chair."

"Oh." Timothy laughed. "Thanks."

Tim stood there another ten or twenty seconds, unsure of whether or not the conversation was over until the man, who was now wearing the headphones again, gave Timothy a sideways glance that seemed to mean that he wanted Timothy to scram.

Tim put the key in his left pocket, then reached into his right pocket and hit the middle button on his cell-phone's number pad to stop the recording. He jogged across the library towards the bathroom, eager to listen to the recording so he could begin writing about the experience.

One of the stall doors was closed in the bathroom, so Tim approached it and stuck his eye up to the crack between the stall-door and the wall.

He saw a man sitting on the toilet with his pants around his ankles and quickly backed away.

Too flustered to think of another place to listen to the recording besides the bathroom, Tim entered the stall next to the man's, locked the door, took a seat on the toilet, and waited for the man to leave the bathroom. When the man did leave Timothy pulled the phone from his pocket and listened to the recording. It was too muffled to be of any use. But no bother. That would be just another interesting aspect of the story he would write—a story that would strongly resemble the one being read (because it is the one being read).

Tim walked back into the library and took a seat in a wooden chair at a desk outside of the reading room. The reading room and cushioned chairs had been bad luck for him today. He'd spent thirty toilsome minutes in the chair by the biographies writing nothing of any substance that morning, and then another hour and a half in a cushioned reading room chair doing just about the same. (Although there was one period during that hour and a half in which Timothy got on a sort of roll and wrote a nice couple paragraphs. The paragraphs that he wrote were so nice in fact that he decided to copy and paste them into a parenthesized portion of the story he was writing about his car key.

Copied and pasted below are the paragraphs that Timothy wrote earlier in the day about his time at the library:

*"I'd rather be bitten by a thousand snakes—heck, a thousand **spiders**— than have writers block," Tim thought to himself.*

*He stood from his chair and bent backwards, stretching his back. He spotted a little piece of black plastic on the ground beside his foot, bent forward, and grabbed it in his hand. He stayed bent forward for a few moments before rising up, hoping that the girl with the turquoise toenails would take notice of his flexibility, because he was proud of his flexibility. Standing up straight he surveyed the plastic in his hands. It was not plastic, but rather it was charcoal and had just looked like plastic. It was a type of charcoal used for drawing. Timothy recognized this because he'd taken an art class during his junior year of high school. There had been a few noteworthy incidents in that class, but none as noteworthy as this one incident that had occurred in another art class, which he'd taken back in middle school, in which he had cut a snippet of a blonde boy's hair off. It was the boy that Timothy had sat beside in that class and whom he had admired at the time, and he cut the hair because he could tell the boy was thinking embarrassing thoughts about him since he'd just screwed up his art project by unsuccessfully attempting to add a beautiful glitter flourish. He'd cut the boys hair with scissors, and immediately felt guilty for it.*

*So he knew the plastic was charcoal.)*

After Timothy copied and pasted those paragraphs, he noticed that his computer was running low on battery, took it with him to a chair near an outlet in the Teen Zone, and began charging it. But by then he'd really written all that he wanted to write, and so he sat there a moment before looking up at the ceiling tiles above. He began to count the dots in the tiles but stopped immediately. It would have been a fruitless task. He turned his attention instead to the papers on the wall. The wall was about ten feet away, and he could only read the words **Series of the Month**, **Staff Favorite of the Month**, and **Staff Favorite of the Month** again. So he rose from his chair and approached the wall. The writing on these papers only held his interest for about twenty seconds, as the writing had only to do with immature teenybopper books, probably because he was in the Teen Zone.

He sat back down and typed a paragraph on his laptop. When he was finished with the paragraph he looked to his right at a very large woman who was standing about seventeen feet away and holding up the fourth Harry Potter book (Harry Potter and the Goblet of Fire) for her young daughter in the pink blouse.

"That's a very good book," Timothy said to the woman.

She looked over her daughter's shoulder at Timothy, and a moment later the daughter turned to look as well.

"I've read all the Harry Potters. Um, that one's actually my favorite."

"Yeah she's read the first three," the woman said.

The daughter nodded in agreement, but Timothy knew the lady was telling the truth anyways.

"Well a lot of people say the fourth one is the best..." said Tim.

The girl nodded again, and the mom said, "Yeah, I haven't read them, but she likes them."

"I've written, um, Harry Potter fan fiction."

Timothy kept saying 'um' because his mind was reeling.

"What's that?" the lady asked.

"I wrote a story once about Harry Potter going back to Hogwarts for college. Just, um, just for fun. I used the real characters and made up a story. Because I'm a writer."

"Ahhh, that's good," said the lady, nodding with modest interest before turning and disappearing behind a row of books with her daughter.

Timothy turned to the laptop on his lap, typed and typed about his interaction with the large woman, and did not look up until he saw an Asian female walking down the book aisle in his direction. She stopped, squatted down, and began to scan the books at the bottom of the shelf. They were anime books. Timothy had never read anime, but couldn't really see himself getting into it.

After typing a paragraph about the Asian (possibly Asian-American, most likely) female Timothy figured that it was probably time to wrap things up. He decided to end the typing session by writing the following two sentences...

Timothy knew it would be a good day. His uncle was in town and would be waiting for him at the house, where they would surely have a fun time playing cards deep into the night.

"Sex change operation for animals...? Would there be a market for it...? No."

Timothy was thinking up inventions and ideas to write about.

"An amusement park where people can give you medicinal shots... Would there be a market for it...? Maybe, but the wrong kind......... The innumerable benefits of hard work... That's a good topic. I'll write about that."

Timothy opened a Word document and spent ten minutes trying to write a decent essay about the benefits of hard work. He got five or six sentences down, but only two of them were good. (*If a man finds a clod of dirt outside on the sidewalk leading up to his house and he picks it up, he can toss that dirt to the side, or he can put it in his garden. It is the little things that count.*) He deleted the Word document and opened back up the one he'd previously typed a couple ideas in. He was not in the least bit discouraged that he'd failed to write a solid essay, for the attempt had just been a technique to get his writing juices flowing, and now they were.

Timothy's understanding of how to get his own writing juices flowing was a result of much hard work. He'd spent many hours of the past year writing a book, and his writing abilities and his understanding of how to make the most of those abilities had improved ornately in that time. Just that morning Timothy had pulled out one of his old note-books and re-read some short movie scripts he'd written in the year 2010. The scripts were almost laughable when compared to the type of scripts he'd be capable of writing now.

After typing a paragraph that he hoped would demonstrate the bene-fits of hard work, Timothy re-read everything he'd written in the Word document and when he got to the second sentence of the last para-graph he right clicked on the word 'splendidly', looked up some syno-nyms for it, and changed it to 'ornately'.

He typed another sentence and then looked out the window and con-sidered what to type in the next. If he had his notebook with him he would have typed up one of his old scripts and put it right in the mid-dle of the Word document he was working on, creating a powerful contrast that would do an excellent job of demonstrating the benefits of hard work. He liked the idea very much, and decided that he'd whip out his old notebook when he got home, type up a couple of the scripts, and add them at the end of whatever he ended up writing in the Word document.

And then his mind began to drift. He'd made his point about hard work, and didn't know what else he should think about.

With his elbow on the cushioned chair's armrest and his head propped up by his hand, he sat and stared at the magazine rack for a good ten minutes. Nothing came. No ideas or thoughts or anything. The sky outside the window was beautiful summer sunny blue, but the breeze of the AC in the reading room was nice and cool. Silence. He wanted to break the silence. There were four people in the reading room—one in each corner, including Timothy, who sat in the back left. In the back right there was a clean fifty-ish man in a faded red polo looking at a laptop, in the front left there was a forty-ish African-American woman with short hair, gold earings, and a hot pink hoodie, and in the front right, obscured by a magazine rack from Timothy's view, was a slender and pretty twenty-ish female with blonde hair, black shorts, a blue work-out top, and a white head band.

Timothy smacked the cushioned armrest of his chair, and it made a muffled *whoosh* noise.

He smacked it again and the *whoosh* noise travelled through the reading room a little more, but the others in the room gave zero response.

He hit it a third time, harder, and this time both the man and the woman glanced up at him (the girl in the corner was obscured from his view and he was unable to observe her reaction).

There was nothing fun about breaking silence, but he decided to write about it anyway, and then he tried to think of something else to do.

But he was unable to come up with anything, and about thirty minutes later he put his laptop into its case and went to the library lobby so he could take a break, sit on the wooden bench, and eat a Larabar.

As he ate the bar a little boy with golden hair and a beaver on his t-shirt exited the bathroom alone, walked across the lobby to the water fountains, took a drink, and then stood with his hands folded behind his back and waited.

Timothy watched the boy, wondering if he was all right. After finishing his Larabar he stood up, threw the wrapper away in the trashcan beside the water fountain, and asked the little boy, "Are you lost?"

The boy looked up at Timothy with his hazel eyes and answered, "No."

"I mean, do you know where your parents are?"

"Um…" The boy nodded. "Yeah. My dad is in the bathroom."

Timothy looked from the boy towards the bathroom door. He turned back to the boy, said okay, and got himself a drink of water. He heard the door to the Men's bathroom open, and turned to see a man in a green polo wiping his hands on his khaki shorts as he exited the bathroom. The boy went to the man, and the man put his hand on the boy's shoulder as they turned to leave the library.

"Have a good day," Timothy said to the boy, who turned, looked at Timothy, looked up at his dad, and then turned back around. The dad half smiled at Timothy, and Tim proceeded through the library to the reading room, where two additional people now sat, and took a seat in his back left chair. There he typed about the lobby and his Larabar and the little boy, and by the time he was finished he did not feel like describing the additional people in the room.

Since he knew he would be typing up his scripts and adding them to the end of this Word document when he got home, Timothy felt no pressure to write a good ending.


*M & M Drama (3) (Drama)*

*[Man] 1: She's mine man. Look you're my brother. I know, but I had her first.*

*[Man] 2: She's mine now.*

*[Girl] G: Wait a minute here, I'm not just some two-bit floozy you can dish around and claim me for a floozy. I don't bend over backwards. I'm an independent woman who can make choices for herself. And let me tell you what. I'm not just going to let you come in here and stomp around.*

*2: Oh look who decided to grow a brain for once.*

*1: Hey. No one talks like that to my babe. Say that to my face.*

*G: I'm sorry. I knew I liked you all along.*

*1: Liked me?*

*G: Oh sorry, loved you. (closes eyes and goes for kiss)*
*1: Hey I'm not that easy babe.*


Bro's (Drama)

*1: How you doing Peter?*
*2: Really excellent actually.*
*1: Oh yeah, why's that?*
*2: I can's say.*
*1: Oh come on.*
*2: She'd kill me if I told.*
*1: Oh so a girl's involved. Oohh.*
*2: Ah jeese. I blew it.*
*1: You kissed Amber didn't you?*
*2: She's going to kill me.*
*1: Calm down I won't tell you told.*
*2: If you do I'll never speak to you again.*


Love (Intimate)

*G: Hey stranger.*
*B: Hey you.*
*G: You haven't called in a while.*
*B: I've been busy.*
*G: Too busy for me? (she moves closer)*
*B: I didn't say that.*
*G: Well how would you feel about dinner?*
*B: I don't know. 6:00 at Joe's.*
*G: You're so smooth.*
*B: Well sand paper tends to do that.*

In a stack on the desk beside Timothy's cushioned chair sat three books that he'd taken from the 'Free Bookshelf'. The middle one was about Cairn Terriers, the top one about female golfers, and the bottom one was a family medical guide. He'd flipped through the female golf one back at the shelf at the front of the library, and had actually found it to be more interesting than he'd expected. Really it was about an older black man named Harvey Penick, who loved teaching women how to golf. Timothy knew this because he'd read the introductions, and then a few pages after that. He knew nothing about the other two books, so he'd give them a look and then decide which of the three he'd like to take home.

He slid the golf book from the top of the stack and picked up the Terrier book beneath. Flipping through the pages, he found that nothing caught his interest whatsoever. He reached the end, looked briefly at the description on the back, decided to flip through it one more time, and this time through his attention was captured by a chapter titled 'Responsible Breeding'. Intrigued, he began to read. But as he did so, his eyebrows furrowed and his intrigue turned to repulsion. The contents of the chapter were much more scientific and grotesque than he'd expected. (Then again, what had he been expecting? Honestly, he hadn't thought about it much. He'd just been intrigued.)

He shut the book and placed it in his lap. Soon he found himself staring into the brown puppy eyes of the Terrier on the cover. He looked down at the wet little nose. Then beneath the nose at the petite mouth. And as he focused on the shiny grey-brown fur, which hung from the Terrier's face like strings of spaghetti, he felt a longing like nothing else to pet the irresistible little dog. Timothy liked this Terrier book.

He held it again in his hands and then, after a moment or two, placed it on top of the golf book. The two books formed his 'Consideration Pile', because he would consider both of these as candidates to be taken home. With both hands he lifted the family medical guide and placed it on his lap. It was a big and heavy book that Timothy guessed, based on the title font and the yellowing of the once white cover, was probably printed in the seventies. "If I had my own coffee table, this would look excellent on it," Timothy thought. But he did not have a coffee table, and so if he were going to select this book over the others, it'd have to be for more than sheer aesthetic purposes. So Timothy cracked the book's spine and gave the pages a scan. Basically it was a book of body science, so he ruled it right out.

Tim placed the family medical guide in its own 'Rejected Pile' next to the 'Consideration Pile' on the desk, stood up, stretched his legs, and then tried to look down at the irritated spider bite on his collarbone, but found that that part of his chest was obscured by his face/chin from his eyes' view. He sighed and walked to the bathroom.

In the bathroom mirror he observed the collarbone spider bite, which was a splotch of red, about the size of a quarter, with two white dots in the middle. With absolute gentleness he reached his pointer finger out and touched the bite. This caused the bite to itch a little more, but he refused to scratch it. Instead he grabbed a paper towel from the dispenser, wet it under the sink faucet, and then dabbed at the bite, hoping the irritation would subside. But the more he dabbed the longer the irritation seemed it would sustain, so Timothy stopped dabbing, threw the damp paper towel away, jammed his hands into his pockets, and said, "I won't itch it."

He walked back to the cushioned chair at the back of the library, took a seat, and grabbed the two books in the 'Consideration Pile', ready to distract his mind from the spider bite.

In his right hand he held the Terrier book, and in his left the golf one. The grey-brown Terrier on the cover of the Terrier book gave it an aesthetic advantage over the golf one—which only had a lower-quality black and white photo of a female golfer on its cover—but according to the price stickers on the books' backs, the golf book was worth $3.05 more.

Tim opened the golf book to the middle and read the first sentence his eyes were drawn to. It was a dull sentence about golf technique.

He put the golf book to the side and opened the Terrier one. He flipped through, admiring the occasional dog photo and contemplating the advantages and disadvantages of choosing it over the golf book. He was having trouble thinking of any real advantages or disadvantages, and soon his mind was far off and wandering as he flipped through the pages.

It was a black and white illustration of a woman giving a dog CPR that brought him back. When his eyes happened upon the illustration his mind stopped its wandering and had an idea.

Timothy set the Terrier book aside and picked back up the family medical guide. He flipped through to the index and looked up 'spider bites'. 'Spider bites' was not in the index, but 'spider nevus' was. So Tim began to turn backwards through the book to page 487, and as he did so he found that it was full of all kinds of interesting illustrations of humans, which he'd missed during his first scan through. He thought, "Maybe after I look up this 'spider nevus', I'll move this one back into the 'Consideration Pile'."

He could not find 'spider nevus' on page 487, so he turned back to the index, checked to make sure he'd read the right page, and then turned again to 487 after confirming that it was indeed the correct page.

487 contained the names of three ailments written in bold font, and then two or three paragraphs about each ailment. Spider nevus was not one of the three ailments, which were: **Non-A, non-B hepatitis, Chronic active hepatitis,** and **Cirrhosis of the liver**. Timothy figured he probably didn't have any of these ailments, but began to scan the descriptive paragraphs to see if he could find anything about spider nevus. He spotted the words 'spider nevi' in the symptoms portion of **Cirrhosis of the liver**. Supposedly they were small, red, spidery marks that appeared on a person's face, arms, and upper trunk. This description somewhat fit Timothy's splotch, so he continued to read the symptoms. Supposedly the symptoms were mild in the early stages. As he read on, even though Timothy was finding that many of these symptoms could apply to him, he remained completely calm. Even when he saw the word 'chronic' in the ailment description, he did not panic. It was not until he saw the word 'parasites' that he began to worry.

In the months of November and December (and it was now June), Timothy had spent five weeks travelling through India—a land known for delicious food that can sometimes, unfortunately, give parasites to weak-stomached foreigners. Because he was extremely hygienic, he never got terribly sick during that trip, like many travelers do. But he'd read before about the dangers of parasites (busting out of peoples' guts with no symptoms), and had always carried with him this subtle worry that he might have some in his intestines from that trip (or from his trips to Thailand and Mexico). It was not that significant of a concern for Tim, but it was the reason he began to worry a tiny bit when he read the word 'parasites' under the cirrhosis description.

He ended up reading everything about cirrhosis of the liver, which was about a page total of information. It was very disturbing stuff. When he'd finished reading, Tim just stared blankly down at the page for five or so minutes. He hadn't seen the actual spider bite him—he'd just woken up three nights before with the red splotch on his collarbone—so he really couldn't be sure whether it was a bite or a nevus. When he looked at the two books sitting in the 'Consideration Pile' he found it hard to believe that just ten or fifteen minutes before, his main concern of the day had been which of the two he'd go home with. "And look at me now," he thought. "I'm facing a possibly chronic disease/ailment."

But before his thoughts could continue in that direction any longer, he stood back up from his chair and walked across the library to the bathroom. He leaned forward before the bathroom mirror, holding down the collar of his shirt with his left hand, and inspected the splotch once again. He squinted his eyes and leaned in as close to the mirror as possible, searching intensely, but not really sure what for.

The bald man with the blonde moustache from the urinal behind Timothy walked up to the sink beside him and began to lather his hands in soap. As the man rinsed the soap away, Tim noticed that he was eying the splotch on his collarbone.

"Can I ask you— um..." said Tim, turning to the man "Does this look like a spider bite?"

The man leaned towards Tim's collarbone, wearing a gracious smile beneath his moustache, and answered, "Yep. That looks like a spider bite to me."

"Okay."

Tim looked at it again in the mirror as the man grabbed a couple paper towels from the dispenser.

"I was worried that it might be nevus."

"What?"

"I read in this health book about something called 'spider nevus'. And it looks red, and uh, kind of like a spider bite."

The man thought about it. "Hmm... I don't know. I've never heard of that."

"Yeah. It's, uh, it's a symptom of cirrhosis of the liver."

The man shook his head with apparent doubt. "Do you drink?"

"No."

"Then I don't think you have cirrhosis of the liver. I think it's just a spider bite."

Timothy nodded. He didn't think so either, and having this man affirm his disbelief put his mind back at ease.

The man threw his paper towels away and Timothy thanked him and told him to have a nice day.

Back in the chair beside the desk, he looked again at the books sitting in their stack and told himself to decide which one he'd like to take home.

His brain was telling him to take the family medical guide, but his instincts were telling him to take the Cairn Terriers. And because Timothy trusted his gut, he picked up the Cairn Terriers and took it home...

Actually he did not go home. And actually he did not just pick up the Cairn Terriers book. He picked up all three, walked outside with his laptop case, ate a Larabar, and then walked back in, took a seat in the reading room, checked his e-mails and WebMD, and began to type about how he'd settled upon choosing the Cairn Terriers from the 'Free Bookshelf' over two other books and the health scare that had occurred while trying to choose. He kept all three books with him because he figured they'd come in handy here and there during the writing process when trying to remember certain bits of text.

A couple hours later, when he'd finished writing about his time at the library, he found himself writing this sentence and wondering if it would make sense to include any of his writing from the day before at the end of this Word document.

He thought about it, thought about it, and thought about it some more. He wondered what sentence he should write next. He wrote two more sentences, and then a third.

"Maybe," he thought, "If I explain about yesterday's writings and my thoughts towards them, then it'll make sense."

So he decided to explain.

The day before, Timothy had come to the library and spent five hours attempting to write anything usable for his book. He'd written a couple sentences of promising but aimless fiction, a page and a half of unsuccessful third-person non-fiction, and one or two deleted sentences of even less successful first-person non-fiction. But he had also written four good sentences—sentences that he wanted to be seen. So he decided to put them at the end of this Word document, right here:

Sentences one and two:

*Reader, if I could, I would reach up out of this page and slap you across the face.* That was a line that Timothy had always wanted to use in his book but that he'd never been able to figure out a way to use without offending his readers, not until he had the idea to use it like this.

Sentences three and four:

Oakley, the sweet man with the tulip scented hair, was sitting cross-legged on the Central Park bench, watching the world in front of him as he breathed the daylight hours in, out, and away like a mist. Thoughts would come, dance around the center of his mind, and go as they pleased.

After Timothy copied and pasted the four sentences, he looked at the stack of books on the desk and wondered if he would ever really read them once they were back at his house. Tim knew he could type about this wondering and the thoughts that came after it, but he'd typed so much already, and knew it was probably time to call it quits.

# Afterword

## Sweet City Woman

There we were, cruising across that lake—flying across it—and she—sitting across from me—lifted her legs and rested them casually across my knees. My heart was beating beneath my life jacket, the wind was blowing, and the times were good. She really wasn't a city woman, we were just out in a boat on a lake, and I believe she was just from the suburbs like me, but I love that song—'Sweet City Woman'—and it made me think of her, so I had to title this that.

Her mom was a friend of my aunt's. My cousin and I had taken the weekend trip with his mom to hang out with their family-friends at the lake house. The girl I'm referring to in the above paragraph was a couple years older than me, and she had a friend there with her. They were two very charming girls—so nice too—and my cousin and I spent the weekend hanging out and laughing with them. The girl that'd rested her legs on my knees was named Hannah, and I don't remember her friend's name, but she had blonde hair, and she said that maybe she could set my cousin up on a date with her little sister. We were thirteen and fourteen. We played cards, and we swam, and in the evening Hannah drove us around in the boat—so fast, so free. I also performed a magic trick that they genuinely enjoyed. Even my cousin liked the trick. After they showed us a couple tricks of their own, we went to the pool and played a game called 'stick in the mud'.

"Stick in the mud! Stick in the mud! Stick in the mud!"

You had to say it three times if you were it. It was kind of like 'Marco Polo', but I don't need to explain it. We watched a movie together, and played 'Clue'. We laughed a lot, and we told a few stories, and we just had a good time—a good weekend.


(Sometimes I think that's what life's about.)

Made in the USA
San Bernardino, CA
27 December 2019

62417800R00097